Urban Social Housing

Urban Social Housing stimulates and contributes to the search for strategic approaches to the production, maintenance and management of urban low-income group housing and the historical, geographic, cultural/political and economic contexts within which it is set. It also gives a brief overview of the prevailing existential threats to humanity caused by global heating and viral pathogen transmissions and examines the social, economic and legislative impact of these phenomena on settlement planning and management. The book distinguishes between public housing and social housing (in which individuals, communities and organisations are engaged in risk- and benefit-sharing partnerships with government and management agencies for affordable urban housing), draws on the author's extensive experience in over 20 countries and includes in-depth case studies from Northern Europe, the Middle East and Latin America.

Patrick Wakely is Professor Emeritus of Urban Development in the University of London and former Director of the Development Planning Unit (DPU), University College London (UCL). An architect (AADipl, London), he has 40 years of experience of research, consultancy, teaching and training in housing, planning and urban development.

'Responses to the need for low-income urban housing have evolved over the past 80 years. It is still evolving, influenced even more so now by the climate crisis and the need to consider public health. In this book, Professor Wakely captures the essence of these and other key determinants in influencing that evolution, including land tenure, land use management, financing, and the need for ongoing partnership and collaboration. This book is a valuable resource for those engaged in low-income urban housing and must contribute to shaping future strategies and responses for all role players in this field.'

Greg Munro, Director, Cities Alliance, Belgium

'Departing from the critical distinction between "public" and "social" housing, this book offers a historical account of the evolution of housing policies from the twentieth century to the present day. In doing so, it examines the travelling of policy and legal framings across the so-called Global North and South and the emergence and recognition of collective processes of social production of habitat, adopted in the commodified production of housing through the State and/or the private sector.

Professor Wakely takes us through this journey while looking at why the right to adequate housing cannot be advanced in dissociation from other contemporary crises, notably the climate emergency and the global health crisis that last manifested through the COVID-19 pandemic of 2020–2023. The book is important reading for those seeking to understand the trajectory of different narratives and approaches to today's debates on urban social housing.'

Adriana Allen, Professor of Development Planning and Sustainability, University College London, UK, President, Habitat International Coalition (HIC)

'The recent COVID-19 pandemic and the fast-growing global warming process have both highlighted the centrality of housing and health conditions in urban areas: more than ever, discussion of housing policies is imperative. In an increasingly urbanised world, it is urgently necessary to critically understand the limits and possibilities of the range of strategies aiming to provide access to housing, especially for the more vulnerable groups and for the urban poor.

We must all learn from the lessons already available, such as those so well organised by Professor Patrick Wakely in this important and timely book. Written with precision as a result of decades of reflection, research, teaching and action in several countries, the book articulates information, analysis, and original proposals for the formulation of answers to the global housing crisis. It is a fundamental reading for urban managers, development agencies, academics, students and members of social movements.'

Edesio Fernandes, Urban and Environmental Researcher, teacher and advisor to the United Nations, World Bank and other international agencies, formerly Director of Land Affairs at the Ministry of Cities, Federal Government of Brazil

'In this concise work, Pat Wakely draws on his extensive academic and professional experience to capture the essential characteristics of post-war urban social housing policy development, including recent times. Focusing primarily on the Global South, and drawing on some of the key examples from the Global North, he identifies important lessons for policy makers including key reflections for addressing the new challenges posed by global heating and potential future pandemics. In particular he highlights the critical role of subsidiarity and participatory partnerships between key public and community actors to enable effective policy interventions for social housing delivery.'

Ramin Keivani, Professor of International Land Policy and Urban Development Oxford Brookes University, UK

Urban Social Housing
Global Health and Climate Change Mitigation and Redress

Patrick Wakely

R Routledge
Taylor & Francis Group

NEW YORK AND LONDON

First published 2024
by Routledge
605 Third Avenue, New York, NY 10158

and by Routledge
4 Park Square, Milton Park, Abingdon, Oxon, OX14 4RN

Routledge is an imprint of the Taylor & Francis Group, an informa business

© 2024 Patrick Wakely

ISBN: 978-1-032-73706-5 (hbk)
ISBN: 978-1-032-72126-2 (pbk)
ISBN: 978-1-003-46554-6 (ebk)

DOI: 10.4324/9781003465546

Typeset in Times New Roman
by Apex CoVantage, LLC

To the memory of John Turner, who died in September 2023.

Contents

Abbreviations and acronyms

ALMO	arms-length management organisation, UK
ADB	Asian Development Bank
CAP	Community Action Planning
BEIS	UK Business, Energy and Industrial Strategy
CEDD	Civil Engineering and Development Department, Government of Hong Kong Special Administrative Region, P.R. China
CLT	Community Land Trust
CMDA	Chennai Metropolitan Development Authority, India
COHRE	Centre on Housing Rights and Evictions
CBO	community-based organisation
CDC	Community Development Council, Sri Lanka
COP	Conference of the Parties (of the IPCC)
DECC	Department (Ministry) of Energy and Climate Change, UK
DPU	Development Planning Unit, University College London
DoE	Department (Ministry) for Environment, Food & Rural Affairs, UK Government
DIY	'Do-it-yourself'
FSDVM	Fundación Salvadoreña de Desarollo y Vivienda Mínima, El Salvador
GiZ	Gesellschaft für Internationale Zusammarbeit (German International Aid Agency)
GLA	Greater London Assembly, UK
HCDC	Housing and Community Development Committee, Sri Lanka
HUDCO	Housing and Urban Development Corporation, India
ICT	Instituto de Crédito Territorial, Colombia
HTA	Hunt Thompson Associates
IDB	Inter-American Development Bank
IPCC	United Nations Intergovernmental Panel on Climate Change
LASDAP	Local Authority Service Delivery Action Plan, Kenya
LISP	Low-Income Settlements Programme, Guyana
LCC	London County Council (in 2000, re-designated GLA)

MMDA	Madras Metropolitan Development Authority
NCC	Nairobi City Council, Kenya
NISCC	Nairobi Informal Settlements Coordinating Committee, Kenya
NGO	non-governmental organisation
NSDF	National Slum Dwellers Federation, India
OHSIP	Oshakati Human Settlements Improvement Programme, Namibia
ODS	Ozone Depleting Substance
OECD	Organisation for Economic Co-operation and Development
PabloVI-2	Pablo VI Segunda Etapa *(PabloVI Second Stage),* Bogotá, Colombia
PPPP	public-private partnership
RUSS	Rural Urban Synthesis Society, CLT London, UK
PFR	Planning for Real
SAP	Structural Adjustment Programme, World Bank
SPARC	Society for the Promotion of Resource Centres, NGO, Mumbai, India
SRA	Slum Rehabilitation Authority, Maharashtra, India
SMH	Secretaria Municiparia de Habitação (*Municipal Secretariat of Housing*), Rio de Janeiro, Brazil
SYP	Syrian Pound (SYP50 = US$ 1^{00} in 2010)
TDR	Transferable Development Right
TFWL	Task Force on Water-Land Interface, Hong Kong
UCL	University College London, UK
UDA	Urban Development Authority, Sri Lanka
UBSP	UNICEF Urban Basic Services Programme, Sri Lanka
UNCHS	United Nations Centre for Human Settlements (Former designation of UN-HABITAT)
UN-HABITAT	United Nations Human Settlements Programme
UNP	United National [political] Party, Sri Lanka
UNDP	United Nations Development Programme
UNICEF	United Nations Children's Fund
ZOPP	Zielorientierte Projektplanung *(Goal-Oriented Project Planning)*

Acknowledgements

I am indebted to Edesio Fernandes, Robert Biel, Adriana Allen, Yap Kioe Sheng, Ramin Keivani, Nick Hall, Santiago Moreno and Jon Broome, all of whom read early drafts or parts of the text and gave me encouragement, new insights and invaluable critical advice.

Robert Biel also wrote the Foreword, for which I am more than grateful.

Patrick Wakely
London
September 2023

Foreword

By Robert Biel

1. Significance of Patrick Wakely's work in today's context

This book arrives at a significant historical juncture. Precisely because the issues we face today are both urgent and complex, we need to bring to bear the full weight of accumulated wisdom. For this reason, Patrick Wakely's book is very topical and of great relevance. It draws upon a lifetime of experience by Patrick himself, as well as the wider community of practice within which he has played a key role; and also the 70-year history of the Development Planning Unit (DPU) University College London (UCL). This conceptual framework evolved through a continuous iterative testing in real-world situations. The ability to juxtapose experiences from different regions and eras—from the Sri Lanka experience to Arab States of the Middle East and the Andes—encapsulates the contribution of the book.

Looking more closely at the kind of experiences Pat Wakely discusses, we could say there are three interrelated aspects: (1) resolving actual physical issues of building, design, etc.; (2) developing socio-institutional structures to permit the unleashing of creative energies of communities in conducting such design tasks; and underpinning all this: (3) rights and access to land.

By viewing the field in this way, we remind ourselves always to address these three aspects, not just in isolation but by integrating them in a holistic framework. This is in contrast to mainstream development discourses, which—since they serve the ruling interests—have every incentive to isolate the issues from one another, for example by treating design as a merely technical process distinct from community input . . . and forgetting about land rights altogether!

2. Historical narrative and the longue durée

The deep historical time frame adopted in this book could be seen as an example of what Fernand Braudel called the *longue durée* (Braudel 1958). The guiding idea is, by rooting our analysis in a re-examination of the past, what we gain will actually be a transformative, militant approach to the *future* . . . "going forward by looking back" (Guldi & Armitage 2014). This gives us two things. Firstly, an understanding of *consistent* themes: thus, deprived communities are still marginalised, and this problem is typically manifested in specific and concrete ways: location, transport, sanitation, etc.; in this respect, we need to rediscover an accumulated wisdom within the urban governance, management and planning traditions. Secondly, the process of *change*: this time frame has witnessed several major changes of era, which we can only fully comprehend in terms of their place within a longer-term narrative.

As Wakely fully realises, while the key issues are immediately social—justice, empowerment, etc.—they can only really be understood against a background of environment and ecology. In one respect, this has always been the case, and earlier debates simply failed to notice it. But also, environment is a newly urgent theme inasmuch as (over roughly the first decades of the twenty-first century) we have entered a new climate regime where extreme events will be increasingly common.

Thus, the book can be read in two complementary ways: as a manual of still-valid best practice assembled from many periods; and as a historical analysis, showing the development and change of issues through time, helping us understand why we face the challenges we do today, and the future-oriented lessons that may be drawn from this trajectory.

In the spirit of the forward-looking commitment of the *longue durée* approach, I will now suggest some elements of a framework, within which we may comprehend the logical and historical relationship between the various issues of planning addressed in the book.

3. Against reductionism and simplification

At the time of the foundation of the Development Planning Unit in UCL, the mainstream planning field was ruled by early post-war 'modernisation' discourses. This orthodoxy made certain incorrect and damaging assumptions which had to be critiqued.

Notably, in all regions there was a pervasive discourse of 'slum clearance', and in the Global South this was especially embodied in hostility towards informal settlements. More generally, this approach neglected the creativity of communities, and reflected a broader repugnance to anything improvised or messy.

Since this analysis of the problem was wrong, solutions were bound to be perverse. Together with a number of key figures with whom he worked closely, Pat helped to overturn the ruling orthodoxy. The critique—put forward notably by John Turner, Otto Koenigsberger and others—showed that what was needed was to understand the *actual* processes whereby settlements grew, discussed in some depth in Pat's earlier book (Wakely 2018). And this in turn gave rise to an alternative planning philosophy—which underpins some of the most progressive examples cited (for example in Section 2.1 on Community Action Planning).

Notably, this called for respecting popular initiatives and spontaneous solutions, working with rather than against them.

Underpinning this, there is a more general point of world view: the top-down planning model is wrong because in all systems there exists a kind of emergent order arising from self-organisation; this constitutes a valuable resource, and planners and managers must learn to respect it.

On this basis, we might say that by absorbing the wisdom in this book, we can nourish a new generation of enlightened urban planners and managers. That in itself would not be bad. But in fact, such a formulation would be insufficient. To take the debate deeper, there are two main issues we need to address.

Firstly, the analysis of any social problem can't simply be anterior to its solution. Rather, the solution arises through an iterative exchange between social practice and whatever concepts are formed about it. This is the philosophy of praxis espoused by Paulo Freire (Freire 2005a, 2005b). And more recently, building on the Freirean method, we have Activist Research methodology, which views social movements—or it would be better to say 'struggles'—as being themselves generators of knowledge: it is they who identify 'the problem' and brainstorm solutions (Choudry 2015; Choudry et al. 2012).

Secondly, modernisation's fear of spontaneous 'mess' is part of the broader problem in dominant thinking. This relates to the control paradigm critiqued by ecofeminism (Merchant 1980): a futile quest to simplify systems to render them predictable, which is the antithesis of true resilience. Complexity, the basis of emergent order, is thereby ruled out.

In urban development/planning there are many concrete cases where a wrong analysis of a single cause has given rise to a false idea of a simple magic bullet (c.f. for example, Badami 2023). However, the point is that it's not just that the wrong cause/bullet was identified but that complex systems are *inherently* not amenable to this kind of approach: they require a different conceptual language, not accessible to a reductionist mindset.

4. Towards a biophilic cybernetics

The earlier argument suggests the need for an alternative conceptual framework of planning/design, against which we can assess the myriad practical examples addressed in this book, incorporating many of them as plugins, but also critiquing certain wrong tendencies which may lurk within them. This should be a perspective which embraces complexity rather than fearing it. What might its principles be?

The starting point could be a more fundamental definition of the *longue durée*, that is, indigenous perspectives which re-connect us with the deep time of humans' mutually transformative relations with their environment. This is intrinsically about a continuing, iterative past-future dialogue (Harjo 2002). Traditional, pre-colonial societies—especially those less stratified on a class/cast basis—developed a mutually transformative partnership between humanity and nature, embodied in natural-seeming forest ecosystems which are effectively 'built environments'; so here again, we find the notion of 'thinking back to look ahead' (c.f. Cooper & Isendahl 2014).

The most important feature of such systems is that they are inherently resilient because they are self-healing, embracing disruption in order to grow stronger, using complexity to generate corrective feedbacks (c.f. Heylighen 2008).

When we transpose this to artificial built systems, that is, cities, two issues arise: treating nature as a paradigm from which to derive artificial analogues (i.e. biomimicry), for example the whole issue of industrial ecology as a framework for circular systems; and ensuring we remember that nature itself is still present within the city and, importantly, its *region*.

This is partly a feature of the mixed socio-ecological character of the city, viewing "cities as hybrid phenomena that emerge from the interactions between human and ecological processes" (Alberti 2008, p.6). But underlying all this is the crucial point that it's neither desirable nor possible to impose a simplified order upon complex, multi-equilibria systems (c.f. Alberti 2008, p.24).

This provides a framework for understanding the social issues, which are our key focus in this debate. From the complexity perspective, we can learn that society too can self-organise. This looks in the direction of using nature-inspired solutions to link physical and social systems, with concepts such as 'panarchy' applicable to both (Gunderson & Holling 2002). A key goal is to identify the faculties of redundancy and self-repair, and any systems which lack this faculty will fail, whether in urban design, housing, etc. (c.f. Boxall 2018).

To work in this way requires a different mode of thinking. The role of the planner could be not to control, but rather to exercise—borrowing a term from cybernetics—'steerage'.

In fact, the need for a socially conscious nature-inspired systems approach has been spotted at various times: at the time of the Russian Revolution, by Aleksander Bogdanov (Bogdanov 1996 [1913–17]); in the work of Edgar Morin (Morin 1992 [1977]); and in the UK, Colin Ward, who explicitly referenced cybernetics (Ward 1973). However, this approach has not quite received the attention it deserves, notably in its application to urban systems. It could be fascinating to interpret the many examples addressed by Wakely, for instance 'Planning for Real', as inputs to such a project.

The goal is to obtain systems which maintain their own resilience by embracing shocks to enhance their self-healing capacity. For this, a key tool is corrective feedbacks. Thus, Donnella Meadows, lead author of the famous *Limits to Growth* report, rightly argued that "a complex system usually has numerous negative feedback loops it can bring into play, so it can self-correct under different conditions and impacts" (Meadows 1999, p.5).

However, in applying this perspective to planning and urbanism, Meadows made a fatal mistake, getting carried away to a point where she strongly praises the argument of systems analyst Jay Forrester, that tearing down subsidised low-income group housing will make the city "better off" (Meadows 2008, p.146). The error was to assume that corrective feedbacks are somehow merely an impersonal 'property' of systems. In reality, they must be exercised by the people at the frontline of resistance against both exploitation and environmental injustice, that is, the corrective is 'struggle'. It is against this background that we could appraise Wakely's many examples, and hopefully develop a dialogue between complex systems theory, algorithmics in modern IT and 'Planning for Real'.

5. The core-periphery dimension

A core/periphery division exists within cities everywhere in the world, and is fundamental to their political ecology: privileged areas tend to entrench a self-reinforcing pattern, whereby insecurity and environmental hazard are exported to deprived areas within each city (here, we are using 'core' in the sense of a locus of dominance and privilege, although it may or may not be located physically in the city centre).

At the same time, we must always be aware that the core/periphery division is fundamentally manifested at an *international* level, embodied in an exploitative system which developed through the centuries-long impetus of colonialism and racism. This is why the geographical focus of Pat's book on cities, in what is conventionally called the Global South, is important.

In this context, the long time frame invites us to consider the conditions of an *evolving* international capitalism. In early colonialism, colonies and semi-colonies were typically prevented from industrialising. But J.A. Hobson's argument predicted that the twentieth century would inaugurate a period when development in the peripheries would be necessary for the continued vitality of international capitalism (Hobson 1902). The challenge for the historic core (the white world of the Global North) would be to seek ways to remain in control of this process (Biel 2000, 2012).

The urban-development implications of the core-periphery issue was explored in an interesting way in another equally prescient work contemporaneous with Hobson, that of Dadabhai Naoroji, who proposed the concept of 'drain' (Naoroji 1962 [1901]): in a colonial context, cities oriented towards the world-economy would lose their rootedness in their own historic, rural and cultural framework. But how would this pan out in a post-colonial context?

Over the twentieth to twenty-first centuries, we can see the unfolding of these issues against the background of successive phase-changes in the international political economy. An important way of conceptualising these changes is the notion of Kondratiev waves in socio-economic organisation (Kondratiev 1935 [1926]), which are phases of international capitalism marked by specific technologies, energy sources, modes of social organisation and of international relations; the 'wave' paradigm was indeed a key point of reference for Braudel's original framework (Braudel 1958).

This perspective clearly has implications—which deserve further research—for urban development too; for example, in more recent phases, the discourse of urbanisation-as-a-problem has given way to affirming cities as 'powerhouses' of the global economy.

The challenge to the historic core's dominance typically references the notion of 'advantage of the latecomer', which is in fact closely linked with the wave model, inasmuch as a country might grasp the emergent characteristics of the approaching wave much more consistently, and sooner, than an entrenched 'old' industrial power.

And a radically new element is thrown into this picture more recently, with the realisation that the next 'wave' will have to be 'green'.

Mainstream versions of green-wave argument are typically framed in a palliative way comforting to capitalism (e.g. Hargroves et al. 2009), and of course, this argument risks being hijacked as an excuse for the core to clean up its act, conveniently exporting the entropy it generates to the periphery, that is, the pollution and emissions from manufacture, or processing of electronic waste. On the other hand, there is an appealing hypothesis that the Global South could gain more autonomy by 'tunnelling' through the environmental Kuznets curve, in other words avoiding the stage of high-polluting industrialisation. Aromar Revi frames this in a very interesting way, as fundamental to the whole urban endeavour, by linking the green transition with improvement in the Human Development Index (Revi 2012).

But of course, all this would have to be made relevant to the exploited populations, in terms of where their lives are really at. The downside of the 'city-powerhouse' discourse is that it heightens the alienation of deprived and marginalised sectors, both in the rural small-town world and in the city itself. This alienation is exploitable by reactionary nationalism, obscurantism and manipulated populist discourses of national identity; for sure, these phenomena are partly rooted in the urban-rural and intra-urban divide.

In the UCL-DPU's history, Michael Safier's work farsightedly emphasised the importance of discovering a new basis for cosmopolitanism (Safier 1996); and in today's rapidly changing situation, such a project finds renewed urgency. Pat Wakely's book plays a really interesting role in this context, by framing history in a manner radically different from the populist discourse, presenting it rather as a history of communities struggling for empowerment.

6. The shift of agendas to (and within) neo-liberalism

It should be obvious that the quest for a viable philosophy of planning/design must dare to critique dominant orthodoxies. But in doing this, we must always be vigilant: ruling discourses are periodically shape-shifting, and in so doing, often subsume and pervert the criticisms of their earlier forms.

Thus, modernisation was quite a controlling discourse associated with a stronger state role. In opposition to this, Friedrich von Hayek developed a right-wing appropriation of complex systems theory, by identifying the paradigm of self-organisation with laissez-faire (Hayek 1964). Once neo-liberalism came in, and notably its expression in the field of development economics (Toye 1993), this argument could serve to justify privatising previous common resources (such as water) and liquidate the public realm, thus drawing fresh swathes of economy into the sphere of private accumulation.

Against this backdrop, while of course it remains valid to critique the 'slum clearance' discourse, we must be aware that social housing built under the hegemony of modernisation did embody an extension of the public realm, both physically and in the commitment of the state to 'provide'. By attacking this, neo-liberalism made it possible to open up all these resources to the depredation of speculative capital and so-called 'developers'.

Nor has the neo-liberal era itself been homogenous, but has rather made itself a moving target, shifting its discourse from time to time. When initially it referenced the atomised selfish individual, it was vulnerable to the accusation that this neglected the role of the social fabric. Accordingly, the ruling ideology adapted to subsume and manipulate all sorts of issues around 'community', resilience, self-help, the miraculous ability of humans to improvise solutions, and hold the social fabric together by non-monetary means. Demands for the recognition of the informal economy (ignored under the modernisation paradigm) could feed into arguments like Hernán de Soto's theory of 'dead capital' (de Soto 2001), which notably exploited women's capacity while pretending to empower them. At an institutional level, 'NGOs' and 'social movements' can be manipulated in many ways to serve the international sociopolitical goals of the historic core (Hearn 2001).

Therefore, we must remain aware that an argument which is radical and progressive in one context could be twisted into its opposite. Such questions can't really be resolved abstractly, but only in the concrete; which is precisely why a critical examination of the kinds of projects referred to in this book can be so valuable.

Surveying the neo-liberal era overall, we might say that, following its initial two phases (market fundamentalism, manipulated discourses of empowerment), a third phase followed the finance crisis of 2008. Society was hollowed out in order to prop up finance capital (i.e. 'austerity'), and the most vulnerable sectors ruthlessly squeezed. Whatever correctives might have existed to inhibit the polarisation of more wealth into fewer hands have disappeared.

This watershed also coincided with a shift of climate regime marked by the prevalence of extreme events. And ecological disaster, together with the finance crisis, became interlocked in extremely perverse ways, notably the shift of parasitic capital into land, whether 'land grabs' to profit from future food shortages, or (of particular relevance to cities) speculation on urban real estate.

From an institutional point of view, this new context calls into question many comforting assumptions that might have been made previously about the merits of subsidiarity, 'arms-length management', etc. Certainly, in the London context, one of the main modes of accumulation is predation by 'developers', itching to demolish social housing; and sadly, local office-holders are only too eager to facilitate this in exchange for the promise of lucrative jobs with those

same developers—calling to mind Lenin's phrase about "accomplices in ban-
ditry", aiming for a "share in the loot" (Lenin 1965 [1920], pp.23, 24).

7. Towards new urban regimes, uniting sustainability and social empowerment

Once aware of the complexity of this shifting ideological and institutional
backdrop, we should be able to identify those principles within the radical
urban planning tradition which retain their relevance and can form the basis
for a strategy going forward. The principle of bottom-up self-organisation,
despite its attempted hijacking by neo-liberalism, remains valid and important,
embodied in approaches of bricolage, knowledge sovereignty, traditional housing design, jugaad, technology-blending; this diffused process of innovation
accesses the creative edge of chaos (Radjou et al. 2012), and is disruptive in a
sense antithetical to the phoney discourse of tech-billionaires. At the same time,
some definition of the public realm inherited from the statist models should be
defended and built upon.

The question is, can we somehow integrate these different aspects in a way
where each will strengthen the other? Here, the notion of Foundational Economy (c.f. Bentham et al. 2013) can be a useful concept, because it's rooted in
defence of the public realm, while also being open to continuing debates about
how to frame community responses in a way which can't so easily be co-opted.

A strength of Wakely's book is that the COVID experience is a frequent
reference point. And indeed, in opposition to current trends to trying to get back
to 'normal', we really must learn from this trauma in order to emerge stronger.
A key aspect is undoubtedly what it revealed about how society was *already*
sick: this implies a societal definition of pathology (c.f. Smith 2017). While
in an immediate sense the pandemic reflected the depletion of biodiversity in
nature—and with it, the loss of self-regulating corrective responses—this also
serves as an analogy for everything which is wrong with simplified and controlled systems more generally, including urban ones.

If the old institutional measures like subsidiarity have revealed their vulnera-
bility to co-option, we could look to alternative frameworks, notably commons.
Again, these are issues which can't be affirmed in the abstract, and we have
to look at concrete cases. Wakely rightly highlights the need to ask critically
whether a certain project for a community land trust is a hidden way of depleting public land. These are exactly the kind of questions we must always ask.

But fundamentally, the importance of commons is to establish a thread linking to what we could call the 'long *longue durée*' of human history, that is,
Indigenous institutional modes (c.f. Escobar 2018),

And this in turn brings us to one of the most important principles which
may serve to connect commons with the Foundational Economy, that is, the
notion of care. It is true that neo-liberalism tries its best to parasitise upon
care, or "free-riding on the lifeworld" (Fraser 2016). But there exists a way of
framing care which consciously resists this. Thus, the recent work of Fleury

and Fenoglio seeks to identify that element which "can't be robbed" (Fleury & Fenoglio 2022). This notably connects the design of buildings with a broader, systemic definition of care which directly addresses the current sick pathology. Throughout this argument, the notion of commons serves as a unifying theme. Once again, the criterion of agency remains paramount. Who are the communities who should be served? Speaking of 'the poor', as many mainstream development discourses do, is inadequate or even reactionary if it pretends this is merely a 'condition' and hides the reality that people are exploited. 'Working class' could be an improvement. But the key issue really comes in with intersectionality. This connects us with complexity as a source of strength. It is also the way struggles are *really* manifested, as revealed in the activist scholarship paradigm (Choudry et al. 2012). In this argument, 'organisation' is both a process of militance, and a building block of order-formation at a societal level.

Robert Biel

References

Alberti, M. 2008 '*Advances in urban ecology—Integrating human and ecological processes in urban ecosystems*', Springer Science.
Badami, M. 2023 '*Compressed natural gas buses in India: Seeing through the air pollution lens, darkly*', Seminar presentation, UCL Development Planning Unit (June).
Bentham J. et al. 2013. *Manifesto for the Foundational Economy*. Manchester: Centre for Research on Socio-Cultural Change (CRESC) Working Paper no. 131.
Biel, R. 2000 '*The new imperialism*', Zed Books, London.
Biel, R. 2012 '*The entropy of capitalism*', Brill, Leiden.
Bogdanov, A. 1996 [1913–17] '*Bogdanov's Tektologia [original title: The universal science of organisation (Tektologia)]*', Centre for Systems Studies Press, Hull, UK.
Boxall, S. 2018 '*The London plan—doomed to fail because it's impossible to deliver?*', Nov.11, https://stevenboxall.wordpress.com/2018/11/11/the-london-plan-doomed-to-fail-because-its-impossible-to-deliver/
Braudel, F. 1958 '*La longue durée*', Annales—Débats et combats, pp.725 ff.
Choudry, A. 2015 '*Learning activism—The intellectual life of contemporary social movements*', University of Toronto Press, Toronto.
Choudry, A. et al. (eds) 2012 '*Organize! Building from the local for global justice*', PM Press, Montreal.
Cooper, J. & C. Isendahl 2014 '*Thinking back to look ahead*', Global Change, No.83 (Dec.)
De Soto, H. 2001 '*The mystery of capital*', Finance and Development, Vol.38, No.1 (Mar.).
Escobar A. 2018. *Patterns of Commoning: Commons in the Pluriverse*. Commons Strategies Group. June 8. https://blog.p2pfoundation.net/patterns-of-commoning-commons-in-the-pluriverse/2018/06/08
Fleury, C. & A. Fenoglio 2022 '*Ce qui ne peut être volé: Charte du Verstohlen*', Tracte, Gallimard, Paris.
Fraser N. 2016. "Contradictions of capital and care" *New Left Review*. Aug. 1.

Freire, P. 2005a [1970] '*Pedagogy of the oppressed*', Continuum, New York.
Freire, P. 2005b [1974] '*Education for critical consciousness*', Continuum, New York.
Guldi, J. & D. Armitage 2014 '*The history manifesto*', Cambridge University Press, Cambridge.
Gunderson, L.H. & C.S. Holling (eds) 2002 '*Panarchy: Understanding transformation in human and natural systems*', Island Press, Washington, DC.
Hargroves, C. et al. 2009 '*Factor five: Transforming the global economy through 80% improvements in resource productivity. A report of the club of Rome*', Earthscan/Natural Edge, London.
Harjo, J. 2002 '*A map to the next world in how we became human: New and selected poems: 1975–2001*', W. W. Norton and Company.
Hayek, F. von. 1964 '*The theory of complex phenomena*', in Bunge, M. (ed) 'The critical approach to science and philosophy', Collier-Macmillan, London.
Hearn, J. 2001 '*The "uses and abuses" of civil society in Africa*', Review of African Political Economy, No.87 (Mar.).
Heylighen, F. 2008 '*Complexity and self-organization*', in Bates, M.J. & M. Maack (eds) 'Encyclopedia of library and information sciences', Taylor & Francis.
Hobson, 1902.
Kondratiev, N.D. 1935 [1926] '*The long waves in economic life*', The Review of Economic Statistics, Vol.17, No.6, pp.105 ff., a reprint of '*Die Langen Wellen der Konjunktur*', Archiv für Sozialwissenschaft u. Sozialpolitik, Vol.56, No.3.
Lenin V.I. 1965 [1920]. *Left-wing Communism, an Infantile Disorder*. Beijing: Foreign Languages Press.
Meadows, D.H. 1999 '*Leverage points: Places to intervene in a system*', The Sustainability Institute, Hartland Vermont.
Meadows, D.H. 2008 '*Thinking in systems—A primer*', Earthscan London, UK.
Merchant, C. 1980 '*The death of nature—women, ecology and the scientific revolution*', Harper San Francisco, USA.
Morin, E. 1992 [1977] '*Method: Towards a study of humankind. Vol. 1: The nature of nature*', Peter Lang, New York, USA.
Naoroji, D. 1962 [1901] '*Poverty and un-British rule in India*', Government of India, Delhi, India.
Radjou, N. et al. 2012 '*Jugaad innovation: A frugal and flexible approach to innovation for the 21st century*', Random House, India.
Revi, A. 2012 '*The opportunity for sustainable habitat development in India*', Presentation, Bangalore, Dec. 11.
Safier, M. 1996 '*The cosmopolitan challenge in cities on the edge of the millennium—Moving from conflict to co-existence*', City, Vol.1, No.3–4, pp.12–29.
Smith, R.C. 2017 '*Society and social pathology: A framework for progress*', Palgrave Macmillan, London, UH.
Toye, J. 1993 '*Dilemmas of development—Reflections on the counter-revolution in development theory and policy*', Blackwell, Oxford.
Wakely, P. 2018 '*Housing in developing cities: Experience and lessons*', Routledge/Taylor and Francis, New York, USA and Abingdon, UK.
Ward, C. 1973 '*Anarchy in action*', George Allen and Unwin, London.

Preface and introduction

This book, by drawing on international illustrative examples,[1] aims to stimulate and contribute to the search for, and implementation of, strategic approaches to the production, maintenance and management of urban low-income group housing through the formulation and delivery of sustainable strategies, based on the principles of subsidiarity and partnerships of local government authorities with urban communities and households. To be operationally efficacious, it is essential that any such strategies, *inter alia*, address deteriorating climatic conditions, caused by global heating and the risks and threats of pathogenic transmissions, by substituting them with sustainable energy generation and the cultivation and maintenance of carbon-absorbing and convivial, health-protecting, local environments.

The broad, popular belief that cities bear the predominant responsibility for, and are inordinately threatened by, the two existential crises that have characterised the decade of the early 2020s is that:

1. the emission of greenhouse gases, notably carbon dioxide (CO_2), are the principal agents of global heating that impact on the lives of the world's population, including town and city dwellers; and
2. the global transmission of viral pathogens, in dense concentrations of people in cities, which also tend to be centres of worldwide exchange between both local and international travellers.

These perceptions are basically correct, though closer examination reveals important distinctions that qualify them, such as the extent of manufacturing and other economic activities in any town or city (Hoonrweg et al. 2011), also the distribution and types of housing that typically covers some 60–80 percent of the developed land and in the order of 50–70 percent of the value of the fixed capital formation of towns and cities (UN-HABITAT 2003).

The existential threats posed by changes in the world's climate and the pandemic transmission of viral pathogens are not new phenomena. The impact of the hominid species on the earth's environment and climate and its threat to them is as old as the species itself, as eloquently recounted by Peter Frankopan in his enlightening book *The Earth Transformed* (2023). Jonathan Kennedy, in his equally erudite book *Pathogenesis* (2023), traces the history of the impact of viral pandemics and epidemics, linking them directly with changes in global and regional climates.

In order to redress the current global climate crisis caused by human industrial and economic short-term short-sightedness, perhaps of greater existential threat than any that preceded it, international conventions and the world's media rightly lay emphasis on the need for urgent action to stem the build-up of the 'greenhouse effect'[2] of the earth's atmosphere by reducing/ eliminating the reduction of CO_2-capture by deforestation, the land-extensive rearing of livestock and the 'escape' of methane by the oil prospecting and extraction and mining industries, also by the combustion of fossil fuels on a macro/global scale (Brown 2021). Substantial investment has been made, notably by the USA and Saudi Arabia, in experimentation with high-tech, macro-scale short-term climate change mitigation measures, such as cloud-seeding to generate precipitation in arid conditions, the firing of particulates into the stratosphere to form artificial clouds that reflect solar radiation before it reaches the earth's atmosphere in order to reduce global heating at the surface of the earth;[3] also, the 2021–23 COVID-19 pandemic stimulated new advances in international cooperation in viral research and the manufacture and, in some instances, the inequitable global short-term distribution of vaccines (Lines et al. 2023).

In the face of such wide-ranging, global-scale preoccupations and initiatives, in numerical terms, the production and management of urban housing seemingly pales, almost to insignificance, in the search for solutions. Even the United Nations Global Report on '*Cities and Climate Change*' (UN-HABITAT 2011) barely touches on urban housing as a producer of greenhouse gasses or the extent to which its residents suffer its consequences and how to address them. This, despite recognising that housing and domestic infrastructure and services constitute some 60–80 percent of the developed land of urban areas and shelter more than half the world's population (UN Statistics Division 2021).

Universally, the production, maintenance and management of urban housing have been, and continue to be, market-based activities. Nevertheless, since the mid-twentieth century virtually all governments, socialist and liberal alike, have perceived the need to intervene in urban housing markets in support of low-income households, who are denied access to the established formal, largely private sector, housing market, by their lack of financial resources. Strategic approaches to public sector engagement in urban low-income group housing have ranged from 'conventional' government-financed and -procured public housing[4] to the provision of financial and/or legislative incentives and 'enabling' supports to community-based construction programmes and projects and some entrepreneurial private sector developers.

A clear distinction is made herein between 'Public Housing' and 'Social Housing'; the former, frequently referred to as 'conventional' housing, being unilaterally procured[5] by state agencies to be rented or transferred to low-income group households at subsidised rates; the latter, social housing, denotes affordable housing, in which low-income group beneficiaries play a significant role in all stages of its procurement and management.[6]

Until the last decades of the twentieth century, 'housing' was commonly seen purely as the product of the architectural or engineering functions of the construction industry, usually to meet politically determined numerical production targets. Only more recently has it been linked to wider social policies and the alleviation and ultimate eradication of poverty and, more recently still, the global threats posed by global climate change and pandemic pathogen transmission. 'Social distancing', a common term, coined in the 2020s to minimise the tactile and airborne transmission of viral pathogens, became a social and physical urban planning principle. However, measures such as this are constrained by poverty that, hitherto, have limited the size of dwellings that households can afford and the building densities at which neighbourhoods have ideally been planned and built, both formally and informally (Gupte & Mitlin 2021).

Figure 0.1 Incremental social housing in the process of development by householders, Ciudad Bachué, Bogotá, Colombia

(Photo: Patrick Wakely, 1985)

Notes

1 Examples drawn from my own professional experience (almost entirely in developing countries of the Global South) and from extensive bibliographic research, much of it drawn from 'grey literature' (research and consultancy reports, etc.)
2 The terms 'Greenhouse effect' and 'Greenhouse gas emission' are analogies that refer to the earth's atmosphere that acts on the same principle as the glass in a greenhouse, which allows shortwave direct solar radiation to penetrate to the earth's surface, but inhibits its longwave re-emission to the universe beyond the earth's atmosphere.
3 Such measures are discussed in some detail in the concluding chapter of '*The Earth Transformed*' (Frankopan 2023, pp.641–658).
4 It is widely claimed that the first public housing provided by a metropolitan government is the, now, Boundary Estate in East London, UK, built in 1893 by the, then, London County Council (LCC) on the site of the Nichol Street Rookery, a horrendous, unhealthy, slum that was demolished and the rubble used to create a central mound (now Arnold Circus) landscaped with CO_2-absorbing shrubberies and large shade trees.
5 Procure = Locate and acquire land or select existing neighbourhoods to be redeveloped (Yap 2023, p.170); plan land-use layout; design and install site infrastructure and services; design and build dwellings.
6 Successful examples exist where 'conventional' built public housing is owned, managed and maintained by organisations of its occupants and users, such as is described in Case Study 3 (page 23) and the last section of Case Study 1 (page 60). This 'hybrid' might be termed 'Public Social Housing'.

References

UN-Habitat 2003 (revised 2010) '*The challenge of slums: Global report on human settlements 2003*', Earthscan, London, UK.
UN-Habitat 2011 '*Cities and climate change: Global report on human settlements 2011*', Earthscan, London, UK.
Wakely, P. 2018 '*Housing in developing cities: Experience & lessons*', Routledge/Taylor and Francis, New York, USA and Abingdon, UK.
Yap, K.S. 2023 '*Upgrading informal settlements: Experiences from Asia*', White Lotus Books, Bangkok, Thailand.

1 Prevailing and emerging policy approaches

As already indicated in the Preface, a wide range of strategic approaches for public sector intervention in the production, maintenance and management of urban housing have been developed since the mid-twentieth century[1] and remain as current policy in different parts of the world. However, since the publication of the United Nations *Urban Agenda* in 1996 and, more recently, the *New Urban Agenda* (UN-Habitat 2016), governments throughout the world have adopted the concept, if not always the strategic practice, of 'enabling' individual householders, community-based organisations (CBOs), NGOs and local commercial enterprises to develop, maintain and manage urban housing (discussed in Chapter 2).

1.1 Public sector intervention in low-income group housing

Direct public sector intervention in urban housing in northern Europe grew out of wide-based political reforms that embraced new welfare policies in the wake of the economic depression of capitalism in the 1930s, followed by the war years of the 1940s and the immediate need in the 1950s to replace or renew the urban housing stock of many major cities destroyed or damaged by the second world war bombing, notably in Britain, France, Italy and Germany. It is widely recognised that in the developing countries of the Global South, state intervention in the production of housing for lower-income households was a sequenced progression of clearly identifiable approaches that began in in the 1960s and 1970s and represented perhaps the single most important attempt by governments to make cities more equitable. It comprised public provision of housing finance, the development of land and the construction of dwellings for rent or sale to households, falling into specified (low) income groups. Ministries of housing and government housing departments and agencies were established for the purpose, which can be characterised as a four-stage sequence of increasing involvement of individual households and communities

DOI: 10.4324/9781003465546-1

in the production of officially recognised housing, leading eventually to the current 'enablement' paradigm of support-based partnerships between government, communities and individual households. At the risk of gross oversimplification, this sequence can be identified within the last three decades of the twentieth century as follows:

1. the public works tradition of government-built housing and slum clearance programmes that, in the sequential model presented here, is most readily identified with the post-colonial independence period of the 1960s in South and East Asia, Africa and the economic and political changes in the Middle East and Latin America;
2. the organised (or aided) self-help movement that was strongly promoted in the late 1960s and early 1970s, particularly in Latin America;
3. sites and services projects and slum upgrading programmes that got under way in the 1970s and continued throughout the 1980s in most countries of the Global South; and
4. the provision of state 'enabling' support to low-income group communities and households to procure and manage their own housing and domestic environments, with or without the intervention of NGO assistance or private sector engagement.

Although it has been discussed at some length elsewhere (Wakely 2018 pp.17–32), a brief review of these stages of policy development is in order here, before starting a deeper discussion of the 'enablement' paradigm, as it provides a useful introduction to the current state of the art. It should be remembered, however, that all stages are still current policy in different countries and cities of the South. Thus, although the passages that follow are written in the past tense, as though the strategies that they describe form a sequence that is now behind us, they are in fact still very much part of the present situation.

Before beginning the review, it is important to realise that prior to these policies, governments throughout the world regarded the production of housing for ordinary people not in government employment, or confinement, as a private sector affair. Such activities were influenced only indirectly by governments through programmes that regulated, in some form or other, the investment of resources in the development of land for residential and productive use. The most common forms were

- land use zoning and development controls to secure orderly and compatible land uses;
- property taxation policies that generated local public revenue on the basis of notional differentials in the distribution and consumption of urban services and to control the environmental quality of different areas of cities;
- rent control legislation to fix rents charged by private landlords so that low-income households could find affordable housing; and

- controls on the extent of individual property holding in urban areas in order both to redistribute the property of large urban landowners to their low-income tenants and to reduce the extent to which landowners could profit from exploiting the demand for housing by lower-income groups. (This measure was confined to the Central and South Asian countries of Iran, India, Nepal and Sri Lanka, and Tanzania in East Africa.)

Inevitably, the impact of such measures on the housing that was built, particularly by the lowest-income groups, was determined by the extent to which local authorities were able to enforce them. Thus, while in upper-income group areas the land use regulations and building controls were relatively easy to enforce, this was not the case in the large and growing low-income neighbourhoods where such public controls were, and still are, virtually impossible to police. Such was the regulatory framework at the beginning of the 1960s. Bearing in mind the caveats already expressed, subsequent government intervention in the procurement, maintenance and management of housing for low-income groups in towns and cities in the Global South has broadly followed the four-stage trajectory summarised earlier.

The public works tradition of government-built housing and slum clearance

The first stage, often referred to as "conventional" housing policies, stemmed from the political need for governments to be seen to intervene in the housing market in support of the lowest-income groups. It was also due to a genuine concern for the orderly physical growth of cities and the appearance of the urban building stock. The aesthetic homogeneity of residential areas, to some extent a legacy of the post-war modern movement in architecture, became a symbol of public affluence, good health and social well-being with which governments and city administrations wanted to be identified. It was genuinely believed that governments could provide subsidised housing for all but the very poorest.

The result was the establishment of new public housing agencies or the expansion of existing ministries or departments of public works at the national (or state) level; virtually no public housing authorities were established at a municipal level, with the notable exception of the city of Rio de Janeiro, Brazil.[2] Their first task was to set or adapt standards of space and construction that defined a "minimum standard dwelling" that was deemed acceptable by the professional staff and political decision-makers of the relevant agency. As these officials invariably belonged to the middle classes, the standards, although reduced, were still more suitable for middle-class steady-income earners than the poor. These standards became statutory norms for the production of new housing against which the existing urban housing stock could be measured in order to establish the extent to which it needed replacing, for example, "a minimum of, say, 25m² of habitable living space, of permanent construction with direct access to a permanent supply of potable water and water-borne sanitation".

The outcome of this exercise, together with estimates of residential over-crowding, constituted a notional "housing deficit" which, when added to pro-jections of future population growth and the formation of new households, provided an arithmetical figure of "housing need". To this calculation was applied an estimate of those present and future households that could not afford even the "minimum standard house" at private sector market prices: typically, a very large proportion. This became the basis on which targets were set for the production of subsidised dwellings by the government for the lowest-income groups. Such targets were rarely achieved. For example, in Pakistan in 1972, the Karachi Development Authority set a target to construct 3,000 apartments in the 'Jacob Lines' project to rehouse slum dwellers. By 1980, when the project was abandoned, only some 800 units had been completed. Similar exam-ples from this period can be drawn from countries in South and East Asia, the Middle East, Africa and Latin America.

Such public housing programmes are typified by tenement blocks of minimal-sized apartments or individual single-storey dwellings of relatively high-standard permanent construction with individual utility connections. They were commonly located on the urban periphery where land was available and relatively cheap, but were therefore far from centres of employment and social amenities and with only tenuous and costly transport links. They were designed by government architects and engineers whose aim was to produce the lowest-cost structures that could meet both the standards set by the by-laws and the professionals' view of "how the urban poor should live". There was rarely any attempt to study the particular needs of the intended users, let alone to consult them. The beneficiaries, who were officially qualified by having incomes below an established ceiling or who had been displaced by a slum clearance programme, had no part in the decision-making that determined the location, design, stand-ard of construction or management of their housing. There was therefore little chance that it could respond to the individual needs, demands or aspirations of any of its occupants, and no chance that it could respond to those of all of them.

Official tenancy agreements contained controls that very often extended to the use of the dwellings themselves, for example: "No commerce"; "No ten-ants"; "No animals or "market gardening"; "No extensions or modifications to the building". These arbitrary restrictions were placed upon households that were invariably dependent on being able to supplement small and irregular incomes through such activities, not only in order to feed and clothe themselves but also to pay for the housing, whether it was allocated by hire-purchase of an eventual freehold title or rented on leasehold. And, despite the subsidies that were built into the housing, many occupants could not afford the rent, even though the housing was supposedly designed and subsidised specifically to meet their needs and affordability.

A major consequence of this was that many housing units were sold or transferred by their intended beneficiaries to wealthier households for whom permanent accommodation had a higher priority, either as a home or as a capital or income-earning investment. The official reaction to this perfectly rational behaviour was frequently one of 'moral outrage' couched in terms of the "ungrateful and mercenary" response of the urban poor in using public subsidies ("government charity") with which to speculate. Rarely was it understood or accepted that for low-income households living close to the breadline, the responsibility for real estate was often low on a list of livelihood priorities for survival, particularly when a subsidised dwelling represented a valuable asset to exchange either for a lump sum or for a rent-based income.

In situations where resale, transfer or subletting were uncommon, usually in rental housing estates which had been cheaply built to minimise capital costs, environmental conditions tended to deteriorate very rapidly. To a large extent, this stemmed from the occupants' exclusion from any direct involvement in the location or design of their dwellings, and the consequent perception that they had no responsibility for the maintenance and management of their homes and the common spaces around them. This responsibility was seen to rest with the landlord: the housing authority. However, the public housing agencies were unable to fulfil their management and maintenance functions owing to scarcity of resources.

A slightly different aspect of official low-income housing provision was slum clearance. Although the two activities often went hand-in-hand, slum clearance achieved its own rationale when governments saw it as their responsibility to rid cities of the perceptions of "unhealthy and unsightly slums and shanty settlements" that were springing up at an ever-increasing rate. Slum clearance programmes usually concentrated on the removal of self-built shanties instead of dealing with overcrowded, run-down central area slum-tenements in old buildings which presented much more difficult problems involving complicated ownership networks and issues of design and construction in or close to central-city business districts. In general, slum clearance programmes solved few problems. Accounts involving the destruction of hundreds of thousands of modest but affordable dwellings abound across the developing world. In Asia, for example, as Seoul, South Korea, prepared for the 1988 Olympic Games, world attention was drawn to its long history of evictions and slum clearance to little real effect, involving millions of low-income citizens; 90,000 people were evicted in Manila, Philippines, and their dwellings demolished in a single three-month period in 1964; a 1985 study found that some 270,000 people in Bangkok, Thailand, were under threat of eviction; in 1975–1977 more than 150,000 people lost their dwellings in Delhi, India, as part of a "city beautification programme".

Despite ambitious intentions to rehouse slum clearance victims in new public housing, very few were actually rehoused. Even then, they were often moved to new sites on the urban fringes or beyond, where land was cheap and

Figure 1.1 Khayelitsha, Cape Town, South Africa, official eviction and slum clearance
           in progress
(Photo: Patrick Wakely, 2005)

they were "out-of-site". Such locations were far from centres of employment
that offered work suitable for semi- and unskilled people who then had to spend
a large proportion of their low and usually unstable incomes on transport. In
addition, such new low-income housing areas, typically populated by young
and migrant populations, were often underserved with basic health and edu-
cational facilities. Thus, slum clearance tended to be merely slum-relocation
as households were forced to start the painful and alienating process of once
again illegally setting up their homes in a different place, while waiting for the
next round of slum clearance to catch up with them. There were occasional
reversals of these programmes where communities were sufficiently organised
or assisted to be able to resist them.

   At a different level, public housing projects put a major strain on the construction and building materials industries. These were already under pressure
from other national and urban development efforts. This strain was aggravated
by the perception that investment in subsidised housing for the lowest income
groups was not 'economically productive'. At best it was classified as a politically necessary 'social overhead'. Even in socialist mixed-economy countries,
housing was not considered to be a necessary welfare function of the state, such
as health care or education. There was, therefore, constant pressure to reduce
the costs of public housing programmes or to curtail them in order to release

resources to the more obviously productive branches of the construction sector such as civil and agricultural engineering, transport and industry.

There were two common responses to such pressure. These were either to reduce the subsidies or to cut the costs, or both. The reduction of subsidies meant recovering a greater proportion, if not all, of project costs from the beneficiaries. But this, in turn, meant accepting higher-income groups as beneficiaries, effectively excluding the lowest-income target groups from public housing projects. For example, in 1988, the Indian Housing and Urban Development Corporation (HUDCO) merged the two lowest-income categories in its classification system for loan eligibility, thereby effectively releasing state housing boards and development authorities from having to construct housing for the poorest groups.

Cutting costs meant either reducing space and construction standards below those previously set and politically accepted as "minimum", or reducing the cost of construction.

The organised self-help movement

The attempt to reduce construction costs was the main reason for the introduction of organised self-help programmes (aided self-help). These programmes constitute the second stage in the sequence of public housing policy development in developing countries of the Global South.[3] Essentially, the goal was to organise the beneficiaries of new low-cost housing projects into 'voluntary' work units to build the project. Although project management varied widely, it was generally agreed that dwellings would not be allocated until the end of the project, thereby ensuring that an equal effort was put in by all to all of its parts. Thus, people could not concentrate their energies only on the house that would eventually be theirs.

The principal argument behind the organised self-help movement was that by using its beneficiaries to build the project, labour costs could be reduced, thereby reducing overall costs. It was also often argued that, in addition, this approach would obviate the need for private sector contractors, as building materials and construction supervision (the "aid" to the self-help) could be supplied direct by the public works agency. In addition, all contractors' overheads and profits would also be saved. This, in turn, would relieve pressure on the formal construction industry, which could then be employed more productively in other sectors that demanded higher skill and technology levels than the low-cost housing sector.

It was argued that the collective involvement of beneficiary households in the construction of their own homes and neighbourhoods would foster a commitment that would reduce the degree of speculative resale to higher-income groups. It would also help to develop a community spirit in an otherwise-heterogeneous assembly of low-income families. As a bonus, householders, many of whom were recent migrants to cities with few urban skills, would learn a productive building-trade through the construction of their own houses. Though much was learned and developed from the organised self-help experiments of the early 1960s, the expectations for the approach as a solution to urban low-cost housing problems were short-lived. There were several very basic reasons.

Principal amongst these was the dependence on complex and sophisticated management processes, not only of often quite large construction sites and operational sequences but also of the social interests of participating households. To be operable, projects had to start with a period of social preparation which often meant little to the participating households whose ambitions were only to gain legal access to an acceptable and affordable piece of urban real estate. Even having gone through this process, in many projects, rivalries and resentments arose over the extent of one family's labour contribution in comparison to that of others, or because of a period of unanticipated slow progress in construction, or a delay in the delivery of building materials. This often reduced morale and cooperation to the extent of killing the project before its completion.

The aim of cost reduction through the employment of beneficiary householders as unpaid labour also proved dubious. In countries with relatively low wage rates, the labour component of total project cost of even very low-quality permanent construction was rarely, if ever, more than 20 percent. The unskilled labour component of which was about one-third of the total labour costs. Hence, only minimal savings were generated by the use of unpaid unskilled community labour. In addition, the use of skilled manpower (carpenters, masons, bricklayers, plumbers, etc.) to organise, supervise and train totally inexperienced labour was far less productive than if it was part of a conventional construction team.

Furthermore, the obligatory nature of participation in organised self-help was often resented, especially when compared with the fortunes of those who had received fully constructed, subsidised housing at no, or little, additional cost. For despite their role in digging trenches and laying bricks, organised self-help project beneficiaries rarely had more access to the fundamental decisions over location, design or cost of their dwellings than the occupants of 'conventional' prebuilt blocks of apartments.

Even so, despite the problems and failures of the approach as a whole, organised self-help made an important contribution to understanding the link between public housing production and community development. For the first time, the engineers and architects in the housing authorities were joined by social workers. Their duties were to mobilise and manage the work brigades, but their work often took them well beyond this into the wider realms of community development and local environmental management.

Sites and services and slum and squatter settlement upgrading

The experience gained in organised self-help, together with several other significant events in the 1960s and early 1970s, came together to launch the third stage in this coarse chronology of direct public sector intervention in the provision of urban housing, namely the development of sites and services projects. Broadly, this approach entailed a division of responsibility whereby government provided those components that could not easily be found or assembled by individual low-income families such as land (sites) and basic infrastructure (services). For their part, each household assumed responsibility for procuring (building) the superstructure of their dwelling. Thus, for the first time, it was possible for beneficiaries of public housing projects to take responsibility for more than the most marginal decisions concerning the cost, production and management of their dwellings and domestic environment.

The main advances of the period derived primarily from fresh studies by such people as John F.C. Turner of the mechanisms by which slums and squatter settlements grew (Wakely 2018, pp.1–16). These, in turn, were driven by the high urban growth rates in Asia in the 1960s, which had caused such highly visible solutions to the provision of low-income shelter to proliferate in the first place. For example, in the inter-censorial period of the 1960s, the population of Mumbai (Bombay), then a city of some seven million people, increased by almost 900 new households each week, while Jakarta and Manila were each adding close to a quarter of a million people a year. By the end of the decade, more than half the population of many cities in the Global South was living in illegal structures on land to which they had no title. Not only had they received no official recognition or assistance in housing themselves but they had often been harassed by eviction orders and slum clearance programmes in the process.

John Turner's and Rolf Goetz' now famous paper delivered at a United Nations conference in Pittsburgh in 1966 laid bare the mechanisms by which these expanding settlements grew and were managed. It is regarded by many as the starting point of a new understanding of low-income urban settlements. It was followed by studies of informal settlements in many different cities of the Global South in the late 1960s and early 1970s, which further developed an understanding that, together with a new vocabulary, gradually found its way into official policy.

The main advance was a recognition of the ability and resourcefulness of urban low-income households to produce (or procure) and manage their own shelter and domestic infrastructure. It was demonstrated that home construction is often a lengthy, sometimes never-ending, process that corresponds to the changing demands and fortunes of the owners and users. Although many squatter households did not actually construct their own dwellings using family labour, highly cost-effective solutions were achieved because they kept very tight control on the acquisition of building materials and the management and supervision of construction by the tradesmen and artisans that they themselves employed. Perhaps most crucially, the importance of security of tenure to land (not necessarily freehold title) as a precondition for individual investment in residential development was reinforced.

At the same time, a change in the perception of the role of housing in the process of urban economic development was beginning to take place, together with refinements in the economic and political arguments for public investment in low-income housing. Not only was the relationship between good environmental health and productivity being made more explicit but, with the development of a better understanding of the 'informal sector' as a major contributor to the urban economy, the importance of domestic housing as the site of manufacturing and commercial activity became more apparent. Increasingly it was observed that, given security of tenure to land, even minute household savings were invested in its development. Thus, it was hypothesised that the development of recognised housing in place of illegal settlements would ultimately generate new contributions to property taxes which are a basic source of municipal revenue throughout the world. Furthermore, it was thought that a sense of domestic security would enhance political stability as hitherto disenfranchised people gained a recognised stake in urban real estate and hence a commensurate status in urban society.

Nevertheless, these observations and arguments were accompanied by a growing awareness of the extent of environmental deprivation in the expanding slums and squatter settlements in developing cities. This could not only threaten the health and safety of slum inhabitants but also those of the formally recognised and wealthier neighbourhoods of cities. Thus, slum clearance programmes maintained a high priority on the official agenda, but, in view of the arguments outlined earlier, they gradually gave way to slum improvement and environmental upgrading projects rather than outright clearance.

The basic ingredients of slum upgrading were the award of legal rights to the land upon which squatters lived, and the provision of access to safe water and waste disposal (Yap 2023, pp.1–83). Such programmes often went hand-in-hand with sites and services projects in order to provide new land for those households who had to be moved to clear space for public amenities and use, and safe access.

However, there has been a very wide interpretation of adequate plot sizes and acceptable levels of service provision in sites and services projects. These range from little more than a plot of ground demarcated by four pegs marking plot corners and access to communal water and sanitation points, to projects in which substantial core houses were built by government housing agencies. In India, the vast sites and services projects in the 1970s World Bank financed Chennai (Madras) urban development projects at Arumbakkam and Mogappair provided individual water connections and waterborne sanitation to every plot. However, in order to reach the lower-income groups with minimal subsidies, the smallest plot sizes were as low as 33m².

From 1972, the World Bank played a major role in developing and promoting sites and services and slum upgrading programmes throughout the developing world. In this way it extended its dubious 'principle of replicability'.[4] Although these measures have certainly brought acceptable housing within the reach of many low-income households previously excluded from the formal, 'conventional' housing market, there are aspects that have been questioned. One of these concerns financial responsibility for the capital cost of land and service provision. In many sites and services projects, the infrastructure (roads, drains, main water supply, public open space, etc.) installation cost has been recovered directly from the beneficiaries, whilst in the higher income areas in the rest of the city, the cost of new service installation has been spread across the whole urban population through the local (property) taxation system. On occasion, in order to design projects that were affordable to very low-income target groups without any form of subsidy, plot sizes have been so small that any future development has been virtually impossible. In India, this was the case in the Chennai (Madras) urban development project already mentioned. Also in India, the Delhi Development Authority designed plot sizes as small as 20.4m^2!

However, perhaps the most serious common failure in sites and services projects has concerned the assumptions made of low-income households' ability and willingness to pay for housing. Early World Bank–financed projects assumed that some 25 percent of household income could and would be devoted to housing. This frequently proved to be far too high. Twelve to 15 percent or even less is a more likely proportion when up to 80 percent of an urban household's income may have to be spent on food alone. For example, the Indian Housing and Urban Development Corporation (HUDCO) established and applied a working standard of 7.5 percent for the lowest income groups. However, often, having established a figure for ability to pay, projects have been designed that consume the whole of this amount in the cost of land and infrastructure, leaving nothing with which to build the dwelling. Even where the use of traditional and second-hand building materials is permitted, the construction of a house still requires substantial capital and recurrent payments. And in many projects, the design of the dwellings and construction standards were stringently controlled. The use of impermanent and second-hand materials was not allowed for fear that "a new, government-sponsored 'slum' would be created".

Notwithstanding this array of problems with many of the first generation of sites and services and slum upgrading programmes, the approach represented a significant advance. This was particularly so in terms of householder participation when compared to the centralised approaches of the conventional public works tradition and the organised self-help movement. In the most progressive sites and services projects, households were officially allowed to make and implement significant decisions concerning the design of their dwellings: the extent and rate of their investment in the construction of their houses; the process by which they would be built, extended and modified, and who would do the work—either themselves or a contractor appointed and supervised by them. However, even with these advances, householders still had little, if any, choice in the location of their housing, the extent of land for which they had to pay or the level of services to which they had access.

The beneficiaries of slum and shanty upgrading programmes also gained the security of officially recognised tenure to the land that they occupied and, in the best programmes, financial and technical assistance for improvements to their dwellings. Upgrading projects provided a range of infrastructure and services such as water, sanitation, street lighting, paved access ways, surface water drainage and garbage removal. However, residents' participation was generally limited. In many instances, slum dwellers were not consulted on the type or level of improvements that were being installed and were not involved in its management (Yap 2023, pp.84–195). Thus, it was not uncommon for public amenities to deteriorate very rapidly or even to be vandalised. Quite clearly, "public participation" still meant the participation of low-income households in government housing projects rather than the other way round—government participation in people's projects!

In nearly all countries, sites and services and upgrading schemes continued to be viewed as distinct projects rather than becoming a basis for policy covering all public housing. Indeed, as described in the previous section, special project offices that were independent of the established housing authority or ministry were often set up to manage sites and services and slum upgrading projects.

The Sri Lanka Million Houses Programme, launched by the centre-left United National Party (UNP) government in 1983, was the first national housing strategy explicitly aimed at devolving decision-making to the users of public housing. The National Housing Development Authority (NHDA) changed from being a highly centralised design and construction management department in the preceding national 'One Lakh Houses' aided self-help Programme to become a decentralised agency for the provision of credit and technical support to low-income households and communities (Wakely 2018, pp.63–68; Yap 2023, pp.100–116). It was the first coherent experiment in the implementation of the fourth and current stage in this chronology of public housing policies, namely the 'enablement' paradigm. This will be discussed further in the next section.

The emergence of NGOs

The early 1970s saw the formation of non-governmental organisations (NGOs) and their advocacy of alternative forms of development that were more in tune with the economic and social conditions of the urban poor. NGOs, both international and local, assumed so many different sizes and forms that a generally acceptable typology has yet to emerge (Bebbington et al. 2008 pp.3–38). However, an almost-universal theme within the NGO community was, and still is, dissatisfaction with the status quo. Since this reflects the received opinions of the establishment, NGOs were essentially anti-government in many countries, with those involved sharing a deep mistrust of government (Mitlin & Satterthwaite 2004, pp.3–19).

Within this context, NGO interventions on behalf of the poor have taken two main directions. The first strand was strongly leftist and activist. It opposed the powerful cliques in society on behalf of the poor who were organised to fight evictions, campaign for better working conditions and for redistribution of the benefits of development. It was ideologically driven and often did not focus on actions beyond resisting the establishment. However, by the turn of the twenty-first century, many such NGOs had realised that cooperation with the government and organisation of the poor to meet their own needs was perhaps a more sustainable solution to the 'housing problem' than outright protest. Some have even moved into the sphere of policy advocacy and, in many countries, have been instrumental in changing government policies towards eviction. In 1994 the Centre on Housing Rights and Evictions (COHRE) was established as an international NGO, based in Geneva, with the primary function of opposing any evictions, principally from state-administered properties.[5] By 2012, when COHRE ceased operations, it had active branches in over a dozen countries of the Global North and South alike.

In the second strand, derived from the tradition of charity, the poor have been assisted with the provision of services and infrastructure. The focus being to improve their quality of life through provision of health and education facilities, income generation and credit, and improvement of low-income settlements. While being less paternalistic and more participatory than government, this approach also created a dependency amongst the poor. Essentially led by middle-class activists, this strand was independent of the government but not averse to building collaborative arrangements with it. It has developed towards increasing the capacities of the poor to develop and manage their own situations and also towards mainstreaming alternative development approaches in government policies. (These issues are discussed further in the next chapter.)

Community participation and the engagement of urban low-income households in the planning and management of their neighbourhoods and the improvement and maintenance of their domestic environment and services are now firmly lodged in the international rhetoric of urban poverty alleviation and eradication, also slum improvement, under the general banner of 'good governance'.[6] Almost invariably it is sweepingly assumed that the inhabitants of urban low-income neighbourhoods are members of long-standing and permanent community organisations that are well organised and capable of making collective decisions and cooperating collaboratively to implement them. While such attributes may characterise well-established rural villages, underpinned by traditional leadership structures and social hierarchies, on which much of the theory and practice of community development and participation is based, they do not typify many poor urban areas that provide affordable accommodation to relatively new groupings of citizens in competition with each other for access to scarce urban resources at the same time as having to build new urban livelihoods and create supportive social networks (Riley & Wakely 2005). Outcomes from participatory-based action are influenced by internal factors such as the attributes of individuals in the community and external factors such as education, social norms, and interaction within certain institutions (Ostrom 2010, p.319). Urban poor areas are not homogenous; invariably they are composed of individuals and groups who represent diverse backgrounds.[7] They do not typify many poor urban areas that provide affordable accommodation to relatively new groupings of citizens in competition with each other for access to scarce urban resources at the same time as having to build new urban livelihoods and create supportive social networks (Riley & Wakely 2005). Outcomes from participatory-based action are influenced by internal factors such as the attributes of individuals in the community and external factors such as education, social norms, and interaction within certain institutions (Ostrom 2010, p.319). Urban poor areas are not homogenous; invariably they are composed of individuals and groups who represent diverse backgrounds.

Rapid urbanisation and the deterioration of social, economic and environmental conditions and their consequences in cities of the developing world are well documented.[8] Policy discussions of the mid-twentieth century on arresting urban expansion in the hope that it would contain or remedy such deterioration came to naught. In its stead, urbanisation has been widely acknowledged as the major driver of national and global economic growth, social development and cultural diversity—all positive attributes. In response, global multilateral and bilateral agencies and organisations have actively acknowledged and promoted urbanisation through policy directives, on the basis that "cities are the engines of growth" or "the motors of growth" (OECD 2015, p.15). For the first two decades of the twenty-first century, there has been a proliferation of national and international activities focusing on generating explicit and tacit influence on rural people to migrate to cities, reversing previous demographic policies aimed at discouraging rural-to-urban migration (Bajracharya et al. 1995; Ostby 2015). In the post-COVID-19 world, higher densities in cities may seem anomalous. However, it is observed that the prevailing urban 'problems' may be addressed, in part, by meeting the needs of low-income communities (World Bank 2020).

Following suit, the international 'development industry' considers urbanisation important and has been clamouring for a more urbanised future for developing countries, irrespective of the massive social, economic, environmental, equity and governance issues it has already impacted on these countries (McGranahan & Satterthwaite 2014). But there are dissenting voices that do not question the validity of the call for more economic growth, based on bigger populations in cities, but challenge the entire foundation of the modernist-inspired and Western-experienced understanding of city building, on which current arguments for urbanisation have been based (Murray 2017, pp.93–146; Robinson 2013). Thus, it is more critical than ever to understand what constitutes the community dynamic in urban areas, since there is ample evidence to suggest that the devolution of authority makes the amelioration of urban 'problems' more plausible (Wakely 2018, pp.33–63).

Urban low-income households are not all inalienably individualistic, competitive and uncooperative. They frequently demonstrate a pragmatic ability to come together for mutual support when faced by a common threat or crisis or an opportunity that they can use collectively to their mutual benefit if they collaborate in an organised way, usually disbanding when their short-term goals have been achieved. In several countries in Asia and Africa, this capacity for autonomous local governance and mutual self-help has been embraced by governments, 'formalised' and incorporated in national development policies, particularly for rural areas, though with spin-offs relevant to urban (informal) low-income group communities.[9]

Subsidiarity and the devolution of decision-making and administrative authority are commonly identified as essential ingredients to making informal self-governance and local management a reality (Suhartini & Jones 2019, pp.25–27). Devolution, even in a limited sense, can elevate the effectiveness of low-income group urban development programmes, because it enhances people's control of their own destiny, mitigating the debilitating sense of powerlessness that, more than anything else, is a symptom of poverty, which perpetuates and compounds deprivation (Davidson et al. 1992, pp.5–17).

Following suit, the international 'development industry' considers urbanisation important and has been clamouring for a more urbanised future for developing countries, irrespective of the massive social, economic, environmental, equity and governance issues it has already impacted on these countries (McGranahan & Satterthwaite 2014). But there are dissenting voices that question the validity of the call for more economic growth based on bigger populations in cities, but challenge the entire foundation of the modernist-inspired and Western-experienced, understanding of city building, on which current arguments for urbanisation have been based (Murray 2017, pp.93–146; Robinson 2013). Thus, it is more critical than ever to understand what constitutes the community dynamic in urban areas, since there is ample evidence to suggest that the devolution of authority makes the amelioration of urban 'problems' more plausible (Wakely 2018).

1.2 Subsidiarity

Subsidiarity is the recognition of the lowest effective 'level' of decision-making and action, grounded in the cardinal principle of the participation of those individuals, households, organisations, agencies and institutions most directly affected by the formulation and implementation of development decisions and activities.[10] Its concept and principles underpin the effective management of enabling support-based urban housing strategies, for example: only household members can effectively determine the equitable allocation and use of space within their dwelling—particularly important in the context of 'social distancing' to minimise the transmission of viral pathogens between them. Similarly, the most effective level of decision-making on the design and distribution of neighbourhood open space and landscaping is that of its community of residents and other users. Identifying and planning the location of new or upgraded housing areas within a town or city that will minimise the use of CO_2 and carbon monoxide-emitting vehicles and connect to existing infrastructure and service networks can only be undertaken at the level of municipal government. The impounding and distribution of safe water and extension and maintenance of electric power grids to towns and cities cannot be undertaken below the 'level' of national or regional government authorities.

In most countries, recognition of the principle of subsidiarity and the devolution of authority in the housing sector is an essential starting point. However, 'municipalisation' and the coexistence, even more, the integration, of such alternative policy approaches, embracing measures to mitigate the medium-term impacts of climate change and pathogenic transmission, are likely to pose some fundamental political/ideological contradictions (Fiori & Ramirez 1992). It also invariably calls for radical changes in the management of urban development and the administration of urban infrastructure and service delivery that in many towns and cities require complex and often-contentious processes to ensure inter-agency cooperation or collaboration.

In addition to this collective, interactive learning process, invariably there is a need to separately build the understanding and practical capacity of specific partner groups, such as local politicians (municipal councillors); local government technical and administrative officers; community organisation leaders and representatives. There is also generally a need for community-wide development and management support in neighbourhoods in which partnership-based housing and environmental improvement programmes and projects are being planned and implemented, in order to ensure that all households are fully informed and that effective communication channels and procedures are established and that their leaders and representatives are appropriately and democratically appointed. This is generally a (community development) function of local (municipal) government administration. A disastrous fire that engulfed a tower block of public rental housing apartments (Grenfell Tower) in London in 2017 in which more than 70 residents died and over 130 households were made homeless, revealed the paucity of interaction between the local government authorities (the landlords) and their tenants, a situation common throughout the country. In response, a proposal was made[11] for the national government to provide grant funding to all local councils to cover the cost of establishing and maintaining a 'Social Housing Partnership' in every existing and planned public housing estate in the country. It was proposed that the grant should include the cost of professional/managerial staff, with responsibility for supporting (enabling) the development and functioning of tenant community organisations and leadership as well as 'training' all public and community members in the management and conduct of partnerships.

A similar capacity was established in Brazil by the Rio de Janeiro city government to strengthen and support *favela* (informal settlement) residents associations and consultative community forums working in partnership with the Municipal Housing Department (SMH) in the citywide 'Favela Bairro' upgrading programme—1993–2004 (Fiori & Brandao 2012). For the Dandora sites-and-services project in Nairobi, Kenya, in the early 1970s, the City Council (NCC) set up a Community Development Department to manage relations between the different groups of beneficiary households and the NCC Project Department. The Community Development Department's role in promoting and maintaining strategic links between different fields of action and 'levels' of activity was so essential to the implementation of the project and to its widely acclaimed success that it was made a permanent department of the city administration, in which it has been prominent in supporting the principle and process of subsidiarity in housing and urban development programmes in the city ever since (Lee-Smith & Memon 1988; Riley & Wakely 2005, pp.30–39;).

Notes

1 It is widely claimed that the first public housing provided by a metropolitan government is the, now, Boundary Estate in East London, UK, built in 1893 by the, then, London County Council (LCC) on the site of the 'Nichol Street Rookery', a horrendous, unhealthy, slum that was demolished and the rubble used to create a central mound (now Arnold Circus) landscaped with CO_2-absorbing shrubberies and large shade trees.
2 Secretaria Municipal de Habitaçã (SMH) –Municipal Housing Department
3 Aided Self-help was strongly promoted by the United States Agency for International Development (USAID) 'Alliance for Progress' programme in Latin America, principally Brazil and Colombia, also in some Asian countries, under the Kennedy administration in the 1960s.
4 Meaning: Similar projects should be able to be undertaken without any outside technical or financial assistance and full cost recovery (no hidden subsidies) to the shelter sector.
5 In addition to forced evictions, COHERE had a range of thematic programmes that covered economic, social and cultural rights; strategic litigation; women and housing rights; housing and land restitution; and the rights to water and sanitation.
6 Community participation is central to the United Nations Human Settlements Programme (UN-Habitat) 'New *Urban Agenda*', endorsed by all Member States at the UN World Urban Forum in Quito, Ecuador in 2016. The New Urban Agenda supports the United Nations Sustainable Development Goals (SDGs) 2015–2030, adopted by the UN General Assembly in Sept.2015. Of particular relevance is Goal 11: "to make cities and human settlements inclusive, safe, resilient and sustainable" (United Nations 2015).
7 Ref: the theoretical constructs of Robert Putnam and others (Putnam 2006) and the operational work of Robert Chambers and others (Chambers 2017).
8 See the range of annual '*UN Global Reports on Human Settlements*', 1986–2022 (published variously by: OUP, Earthscan, and Routledge).
9 E.g. The Sarvodaya shramadana Movement in Sri Lanka in the 1950s-70s <https://www.sarvodaya.org>

Ujamaa Movement in Tanzania in the 1960s-70s <https://en.wikipedia.org/wiki/Ujamaa>
Harambee in Kenya in the 1960s-70s https://en.wikipedia.org/wiki/Harambee

10 The adjective 'effective' is key to the concept of 'subsidiarity'. Responsibility is frequently (theoretically) devolved to an assumed 'absolute' lowest 'level' of authority/action, where there is insufficient capability or willingness to undertake it effectively. Likewise, responsibility often rests at a 'level' that is too 'high' to be democratically effective.

11 The proposal was presented to the national government-appointed 'Grenfell Tower Inquiry' and the 'Equality and Human Rights Commission' as part of a composite submission to the UK national Ministry of Housing, Communities & Local Government.

References

Abbott, J. 1996 *'Sharing the city: Community participation in urban management'*, Earthscan, London, UK.

Abrams, C. 1964 *'Housing in the modern world: Man's struggle for shelter in an urbanising world'*, MIT Press, Cambridge, MA, USA.

Arnstein, S.R. 1969 *'A ladder of citizen participation'*, Journal of the American Institute of Planners, Vol.35, No.4, Washington DC, USA.

Bajracharya, B.N. 1995 *'Promoting small towns for rural development: A view from Nepal'*, Asia-Pacific Population Journal, Vol.10, India.

Bebbington, A., S. Hickey & D. Mitlin (eds) 2008 *'Can NGOs make a difference: The challenge of development alternatives'*, Zed Books, London, UK.

Boughton, J. 2018 *'Municipal dreams: The rise and fall of council housing'*, Verso, London, UK.

Burra, S. 1999 *'Resettlement and rehabilitation of the urban poor: The story of Kanjur Marg'*, DPU Working Paper No.99, UCL, London, UK.

Fiori, J. & J. Brandao 2012 *'Spatial strategies and urban social policy: Urbanism and poverty reduction in the Favelas Rio de Janeiro'*, in Hernandez, F., L. Allen & P. Kellett (eds) 'Rethinking the informal city: Critical perspectives from Latin America', Berghahn Books, Oxford, UK and New York, USA

Fiori, J. & R. Ramirez 1992 *'Notes on the self-help housing critique'* in Mathéy, K. (ed) 'Beyond self-help housing' (pp.23–31), Mansell, London, UK.

Geddes, M. 2000 *'Tackling social inclusion in the European Union: The limits to the new orthodoxy of local partnership'*, International Journal of Urban and Regional Research, Vol.24, No.4, Wiley, London, UK.

Gibson, T. 1979 *'People power: Community and works groups in action'*, Pelican, London, UK.

Hamdi, N. & R. Goethert 1997 *'Action planning for cities: A guide to community practice'*, John Ailey & Sons, Chichester, UK.

Helming, S. & M. Göbel 1997 *'ZOPP: Objectives-oriented project planning'*, GTZ, Frankfurt, Germany.

McGranahan, G. & D. Satterthwaite 2014 *'Urbanisation concepts and trends'*, IIED Working Paper, IIED, London, UK.

Mitlin, D. & D. Satterthwaite (eds) 2004 '*Empowering squatter citizen: Local government, civil society and urban poverty reduction*', Earthscan, London, UK.

Murray, M.J. 2017 '*The urbanism of exception: Global urbanism at the start of the 21st century*' (pp.23–45), Cambridge University Press, Cambridge, UK.

Ostby, G. 2015 '*Rural–urban migration, inequality and urban social disorder: Evidence from African and Asian cities*', Conflict Management and Peace Science, Vol.33, No.5, pp.491–515.

Ostrom, E. 2010 '*The challenge of self-governance in complex contemporary environment*', Journal of Speculative Philosophy, Vol.24, No.4, pp.316–332.

Riley, E. & P. Wakely 2005 '*Communities and communication: Building urban partnerships*', ITDG Publishing, Rugby, UK.

Robinson, J. 2013 '*The urban now: Theorising cities beyond the new*', European Journal of Cultural Studies, Vol.16, No.6, pp.659–677.

Suhartini, N. & P. Jones 2019 '*Urban governance and informal settlements*', Springer, Berlin, Germany.

Turner, J.F.C. 1976 '*Housing by people: Towards autonomy in building environments*', Marion Boyars, London, UK.

UN-Habitat 2016 '*Habitat III new urban agenda*', http://habitat3.org/wp-content/uploads/N1639668-English.pdf (accessed Jan.2017).

Wakely, P. 2018 '*Housing in developing cities: Experience and lessons*', Routledge, Taylor and Francis, New York, USA & London, UK.

Yap, K.S. 2023 '*Upgrading informal settlements: Experiences from Asia*', White Lotus Books, Bangkok, Thailand.

2 Implementation strategies

Participatory urban projects contribute more than the material benefits that help in reducing poverty. They stimulate and put in train a transformation that develops capacity and enhances confidence. Poverty can be identified as one of the most potent social determinants with a multitude of causes, sources and outcomes. It is overwhelming and over-encompassing compared to any other determinant when it is chronically deep-rooted in low-income group settlements both in rural and urban areas. In addition to the deprivation of access to goods and services, poverty is also a state of mind. Such multiple deprivation is, at the same time, the cause and the consequence of the state of mind. Endemic poverty generates a self-perpetuating mental state that denies the imagination and capability required for individual dynamism (Davidson et al. 1992; Kämpchen 2011). Alkire (2004, pp.56–67) shows[1] how communities and individuals secure social status and self-respect by ameliorating their poverty through participatory livelihood-generating activity and how participatory democracy at the local level can be truly transformative in rekindling dignity and self-worth to remove deep-seated powerlessness through livelihood-related projects. This is closely aligned with Sen's 'capability approach' to development (Sen 1985; Frediani 2007).

Thus, the will to formally devolve authority to low-income group communities is generally widely welcomed, provided that it comes with appropriate capacity building to enable responsible local governance and efficient and equitable local management, which it rarely does. The level of capacity required by communities and individuals in communities varies and again, as Ostrom (Ibid) identified, is based on both external and internal factors. Thus, one of the basic tenets of the inter-dependent 'decentralisation', 'community participation' and 'good governance' paradigms for urban housing production and management is missing unless adequate appropriate support for its generation/regeneration is provided, not only at the level of low-income households and communities but also at that of the 'enabling' institutions and authorities that support them (Mayo 1993; Cheema 1991)

DOI: 10.4324/9781003465546-2

Case Study 1   Supportive partnership for self-build housing in London, UK

In the mid-1970s, concerned by the high demand for appropriate and afford-able housing, the London Borough of Lewisham in the south-east of the city adjusted its housing policy to enable the participation of eligible house-holds (any resident of the borough who was not a homeowner) to con-tract or construct their own dwellings within the framework of its public social housing policy. There were no requirements to possess any building experience or skills and no limits on age or lack of income. To initiate the new approach strategically, the chair of the Borough Housing Committee was persuaded by Brian Richardson, an assistant Borough architect and enthused by the architect Walter Segal, to instruct the Borough architect to investigate a list of specific sites. The sites were conventionally unbuild-able (on steep slopes, two pieces of 'scrap land' and a suburban garden) but were chosen "to meet the needs of the prevailing housing-needs boom". In 1976, 168 local people on the Council's housing waiting list, or with some need to move into new accommodation and casually intrigued by the idea of building their own new houses, attended a meeting, called by the Council, and descriptively announced in the council's newspaper, *Outlook*, to decide to whom the scheme of self-build houses should be granted. Fourteen par-ticipating families, ranging from young couples with small children to people in their 60s, looking for a new home in which to retire, were selected by ballot and formed into a 'self-build' group, one of them being elected by the rest to be the chairman.[2] Four small sites were selected, and Walter Segal[3] was appointed the project architect, assisted later by the architect Jon Broome. Segal had been instrumental in persuading Lewisham Borough Council's Housing Committee to adopt self-building approaches as part of its social housing programme.[4] He had also informed and trained the first self-builder households in the design and construction processes of his sys-tem.[5] He and Broome were also instrumental in negotiating the acceptance and formal approval of the peculiarities of self-build housing as part of a local government public housing programme.[6] These included both local authori-ties within the borough's administration[7] and those of the Greater Lon-don Council (GLC), which, in 2000, became the Greater London Authority (GLA) and UK Government Departments (Ministries) and Agencies.[8]

The first projects

Work on the 14 houses started in 1979. Men, women, and children all participated in the building process, though there was an option of employing specialist contractors, particularly for technical work such as laying drains and erecting structural frames, also for moving and stacking heavy and bulk-bought deliveries of building materials, etc. All progressed smoothly, with no serious problems. Segal had produced a total of 19 variations of two-, three- and four-bedroom house designs, including both single- and two-story types. However, many of the builder-householders made their own adjustments, additions and changes spontaneously as the construction progressed and after they had 'completed' work and moved in (usually in consultation with Walter Segal or Jon Broome). All 14 houses were completed, furnished and occupied before the end of 1980.

On the strength of the success of the first site, it was decided to develop a second project of 13 self-build houses on similarly sloping land, owned by the Borough Council in Honor Oak. For this project, the architects prepared drawings for a typical two-story house type to which self-builders could choose to add bays to enlarge the dwelling.[9]

Financial terms

The completed dwellings were part purchased by the self-builders and part rented from the Council. Many of the self-builders purchased a lease for 50 percent of the equity with a 'soft' mortgage provided by the Council. The amortisation rate of the loan was reduced by the notional value of their self-help labour to build the house, making the dwellings more affordable to people on low incomes. The other 50 percent of the equity was rented from the Council for half the prevailing equivalent public housing rent for that size of property. The self-builders were able to purchase additional shares of the lease in 10 percent instalments. If they purchased 100 percent of the lease, they could then acquire the freehold under 'Leasehold Reform' legislation. Over a period of 20 years or so, most self-builders had bought the freeholds on the properties because unavoidable rent increases meant that it became cheaper to pay an increased mortgage repayment than the prevailing rent.

Building community

Each self-builder household was responsible for the construction of its own house, though as a group all their new neighbours were doing more or less the same thing at the same time. So, inevitably, through common goodwill, households would help each other out with particularly awkward or heavy jobs, such as raising the main timber frames of the house. Of course, neighbours had to work together on the installation of their shared infrastructure, such as digging drainage trenches and installing sewerage and water supply lines and access ways. So, what started as a group of disparate families and households, who had not met each other before the start of the project, became a tight-knit mutually supportive community, fuelled by street parties, topping-out celebrations on the completion of a house and other such expressions of communal solidarity.

Subsequently, based on the lessons learnt from these two initial projects, further self-build housing projects were developed in South London and elsewhere by local government authorities and independent registered housing associations. Many of these subsequent developments were self-build housing cooperatives for rent, the residents of which enjoyed very low housing costs.

RUSS CLT

In 2009, Rural Urban Synthesis Society (RUSS), a community land trust, was founded by the son of one of the original Lewisham self-builders who built a house in the 1980s as a non-profit, community-based organisation to develop affordable, environmentally sustainable housing, workspaces, and community facilities. It acquired a 250-year lease on land at Church Grove, off Lewisham High Street,[10] from Lewisham Borough Council, at negligible cost, in order to add further to the Borough's public social housing stock.

The trustees of RUSS are its members (i.e. the people who own and live or work on the project land and other members of the public who support RUSS's principles), and ownership and financial arrangements are devised so that they collectively have secure tenure, *in perpetuity,* so that the dwellings remain affordable to people on low incomes. Any change of occupancy can only be between members of the trust. Thus, new occupants have to join the trust and are subject to its rules and obligations.

The site was planned to accommodate 36 one-, two-, three- and four-bedroom single- and two-story dwellings and two four-story blocks of flats, a self-designed, funded and built community hall with a shared kitchen together with a rental spare bedroom for visitors, and allotments, irrigated by impounded rainwater where members could grow vegetables and flowers, outdoor play-spaces for small children and parking spaces for four vehicles—a 'car club'—and secure bicycle storage. The house types and apartment buildings were designed following a programme of intensive co-design sessions with residents and the architects. The buildings were designed as a concrete frame which allowed openings for windows, as required by each occupant. The major works were undertaken by a building contractor, in conjunction with self-build work if residents chose to do the work themselves,[11] in order to minimise building costs and, more importantly, to engage the trust members in the construction of their own dwellings, and therefore their senses of identity with, and 'ownership' of, RUSS.

Components of authority

Frequently, a significant misunderstanding lies in the concepts of 'decentralisation' and devolution, the rhetoric of which is universally prominent amongst the basic principles of urban development projects and local government reform programmes throughout the world.

In considering different forms of participation and partnership in urban development, particularly the development of informal areas, it is important to distinguish between

- governance as a democratic process of decision-making and setting standards;
- the management of new urban development initiatives and capital investments; and
- the routine administration of service delivery and the maintenance of infrastructure, whilst recognising the importance of integrating the linkages between all three.

Governance and planning in a democracy are clearly participatory processes that engage all those who have a stake in decisions that are made, usually through a system of representation, though direct democracy (referenda, 'town-hall meetings', community assemblies, etc.) has an important place in many decision-making processes, particularly those involving, and within, low-income group urban communities, most of which are highly diverse, embracing social majorities and minorities, women, men, young and old, all with different needs, ambitions and allegiances.

Managing the implementation of development plans through programmes and projects, particularly in low-income group neighbourhoods, is increasingly being shown to benefit from partnership arrangements between the funders/financiers (generally government or international agencies), regulators (local government) and the beneficiary communities (Wakely 2020). For example, the administration of service charges for day-to-day utility delivery (water, sanitation, power, etc.) has also often been shown to be more efficient (afford-able) when undertaken, at least in part, by the user community, either in a risk and profit-sharing partnership or through subcontracting arrangements with the service providers. Solid waste management and the maintenance of local infrastructure (street drains, local public open spaces, access ways, etc.) and other community assets are generally more efficient and effective when in local control (Das 2015).

2.1 Participation

The devolution of authority for the planning, maintenance and management of urban housing to the lowest effective level engages community groups that, particularly in low-income group neighbourhoods, are generally ill-equipped with the necessary management and planning skills to take on the responsibili-ties devolved to them. They therefore require enabling supports; frequently pro-vided by specialist NGOs, in addition to local government field-level technical and social staff. To meet these challenges a range of approaches and techniques to advance and support, urban community development organisation and man-agement have been developed, largely through pragmatic, on-the-job, practice with, and by, urban low-income groups, living and working in both informal and formal settlements in towns and cities throughout the world. A consistently successful family of community mobilisation techniques that centre upon par-ticipatory local domestic and environmental problems and collectively gener-ated approaches to solving them and plans for local action to implement them has developed over a period of some 50 years.

It is widely believed that this approach originated from a technique called 'Planning for Real (PFR)', initiated by Tony Gibson in the north of England in the 1970s and subsequently adapted for application in deprived urban neigh-bourhoods in other European countries, notably Germany, Poland and the Neth-erlands, as well as several cities in Argentina, Chile and other Latin American countries (Gibson 1979). Closely related to PFR is 'Community Action Plan-ning (CAP)', specifically developed to mobilise low-income urban communi-ties and strengthen their local management capacity for the implementation of the Urban Sub-programme of the Sri Lanka 'Million Houses Programme (MHP)' in the 1980s (Hamdi & Goethert 1997). ZOPP, 'Goal-Oriented Pro-ject Planning', is a similar environmental upgrading-based technique, within this family of community development and local management support and capacity-building approaches, specifically designed and promoted by the Ger-man development cooperation agency Deutsche Gesellschaft für Internation-ale Zusammarbeit (GiZ) for application to the upgrading of low-income group informal settlements in developing countries of Africa and East Asia, where it has been applied widely (Helming & Göbel 1997). All of the techniques in this 'family' of approaches to environmentally centred community strengthening have a basic cumulative sequence of events in common:

The starting point is to identify and agree a prioritised set of problems faced by the inhabitants of the neighbourhood in question. (This is unlikely to be a single homogenous list, but will be a series of 'problem' sub-groups, faced by different social groups—for example, ethnic origin; women; men; children (boys, girls). With some regularity, the highest priority 'problem' is identified as "poverty and/or lack of access to income earning opportunities and political power". Rarely is the long-term problem of the impact of climate change and global heating perceived as of local importance, except in places that have recently, or frequently, suffered from a geophysical disaster, such as a tsunami or earthquake. The COVID-19 pandemic of 2020–22 that brought acute suffering to low-income communities around the world raised popular awareness of the need for measures to mitigate the transmission of viral infection (Wilkinson 2020).

1. Stemming directly from the collective 'problem-identification' stage, the public discussion turns to agreeing a common 'vision' for the future of the community, its governance and physical environment (neighbourhood).
2. This then leads into the development and agreement of a community 'action plan' that details and prioritises the actions and activities required to solve/ ameliorate the 'problems', in order to achieve the 'vision'. This process includes an examination of what actions and activities can be undertaken by the community organisation itself and those for which 'outside' technical, managerial, financial or legislative assistance will be required, and by whom (i.e. different levels of government, NGO or private sector intervention).
3. The final stage is the establishment of a community-based 'operational organisation', with locally, popularly accepted/elected officers, from amongst the community and, where appropriate, their recognition by the relevant government agencies (Wakely 2020). In terms of practical sustainability, this is the most important stage to ensuring the continuity of autonomous local governance and the management of local environmental quality and the delivery of urban services. This process is invariably guided and facilitated by an individual or agency external to the community.

On occasions, the intentions of such community capacity development projects have been thwarted by the build-up of the community's dependence on the initiating external support agencies, because insufficient attention has been given to the maintenance of continuity after the external agencies withdraw, potentially leaving a managerial vacuum. This is largely due to the level of endurance of capacity that the community has built over the life of the engagement and the effort taken by the engaging agencies to ensure that the community's capacity is strengthened to an adequate level. Appropriate and adequate capacity empowers the community, and they in turn become capable of understanding their rights and obligations, accessing available resources, and ultimately making public authorities accountable. For example, this was successfully achieved in the seminal community-led upgrading of rundown nineteenth century (slum) terrace houses in Macclesfield, UK, initiated by the architect Rod Hackney in the 1970s (Birchall 1988, pp.110–160). It was also demonstrated in the Urban Sub-programme of the Sri Lanka Million Houses Programme (Wakely 2018, pp.63–68), where the 'external' agency support and training personnel made a point of withdrawing 'gradually' and encouraging local NGOs to be called upon by urban grassroots Community Development Councils (CDCs) for advice/help, when needed. As evidence, following the devastation of many low-income neighbourhoods by the 2004 Asian tsunami in coastal towns in the south and east of the country, many CDCs that had been established in urban low-income group areas to benefit from a UNICEF-sponsored 'Urban Basic Services Programme' (UBSP) in the 1970s and the government's participatory 'Million Houses Programme' (MHP) in underserved urban settlements that followed it in the 1980s, and had been left in abeyance for more than a decade, were spontaneously reconstituted by their former office-bearers, to plan and manage local community social and economic rehabilitation and the physical reconstruction of their housing and domestic infrastructure (Hague et al. 2006 pp.43–45).

In summary, the participation of communities that hitherto have shown scant awareness or concern in the planning, maintenance and management of their neighbourhoods inevitably generates local awareness or concern for the medium or long-term impact of global heating, except in countries where extreme, life-threatening heatwaves and/or flooding have been experienced, such as in Sindh, Pakistan, in 2022, or the extent to which physical environmental conditions cause or exacerbate ill health through pathogenic transmission, even in communities in which local epidemics are common. Collective community participation in their identification and amelioration leads to 'folkloric' understanding and, ultimately, their obviation (E&U 2011).

Invariably the introduction of any real participation or partnership in the planning and management of cities and the routine administration of infrastructure and delivery of services in low-income group neighbourhoods entail a degree of decentralisation or devolution of responsibility, and authority has been alien to the occupants of many urban neighbourhoods; also to both national and municipal governments, requiring significant political changes to housing policies and to the administration of their implementation.[12]

2.2 Partnership

Partnerships between municipal governments and administrations, national government line ministries and agencies, organised community groups and individual households are the next stage in the development of effective and sustainable urban housing procurement and management. Participation and partnership have been prominent in the lexicon of low-income group housing and urban development since the early 1970s and an extensive literature has been built up.[13] Nevertheless, Sherrie Arnstein's 'Ladder of Citizen

Participation' (1969), set in the context of the USA 'Model Cities Program' for urban poverty relief and social reform,[14] remains amongst the most useful. Arnstein's analytical model identifies eight rungs on 'the ladder of progression' of degrees of citizen engagement in the development and management of cities and settlements. These are grouped in three broad categories, as follows:

Non-Participation

1. Manipulation
2. Therapy

Degrees of Tokenism

3. Informing
4. Consultation
5. Placation

Degrees of Citizen Power

6. Partnership
7. Delegated Power
8. Citizen Control

Partnership, 'rung 6' on Arnstein's ladder, differs fundamentally from the preceding 'rungs' of limited participation, all of which presuppose a dualistic relationship, in which development and management initiatives and processes are controlled ('owned') by government agencies ('the powerholders' in Arnstein's terminology) that allow users/beneficiaries ('client citizens') varying levels of influence. Partnership, on the other hand, signifies joint control and shared 'ownership' with benefits and risks mutually shared by public sector agencies and beneficiary citizens (organisations).

'Rungs 7 and 8' go beyond joint multilateral control and refer generally to unilateral control by citizens ('the powerless') of particular functions of housing and urban planning and management, generally by the devolution of decision-making and operational authority to user organisations, thereby raising the fundamental issue of subsidiarity, discussed in Chapter 1.

A partnership is a binding voluntary agreement between two or more entities—partners—to join together in order to achieve a common interest, goal or objective, with the aim of thereby achieving a harmonious, efficient and equitable outcome. Though legally backed by agreed 'Articles of Association' that prescribe the particular responsibilities (based on their strengths—skills and experience—and constituency) of each partner (organisation), authentic partnerships are based on mutual trust and understanding of the values, aims, objectives and ambitions of all partners by each partner in order to reach a mutually agreed and respected consensus[15] for planning and action.

Top-down vs Bottom-up

Commentary on partnership within the wider general debate on participation frequently gets into a tangle on the tension between 'top-down' and 'bottom-up'. The champions of empowering the politically and economically weakest sections of urban society tend to argue in favour of the importance of initiatives such as the formation of development partnerships, originating from 'grass-roots' community action. Clearly it is important that such initiatives are nurtured in order to consolidate household and community engagement and respond to the perceptions and demands of those who really understand (from their own experience) user demands and aspirations for housing and local environmental conditions and facilities (Mitlin 2008). However, such bottom-up approaches can consolidate relationships in which the government actors retain a superior authoritarian role that inhibits the democratic equity values of authentic partnership, for example as experienced by the CBO Anjuman Samaji Behbood in the joint venture for the provision of water and sanitation in Dhudiwala informal neighbourhood of Faisalabad, Pakistan, that led to the breakdown of any semblance of the much-vaunted partnership, threatening the implementation of the project that was only salvaged through the mediation of a Karachi-based national NGO—the OPP Research and Training Institute (Alimuddin 2004).

By contrast, where community organisations join a formal public sector initiative clearly based on the principles of authentic partnership at the behest of government, all partners inevitably start off on an equal footing grounded on mutualism and (some) mutual respect (Mackintosh 1992; Hastings 1996). Thus, it is argued that the onus for forming any decision-making partnership for low-income group housing projects or urban development programmes rests with the appropriate agency of local government that, as is indicated later and in Case Study 1 earlier, also bears responsibility for the provision of support and capacity building to enable the effective functioning of sustainable partnerships. Of course, the formation of a development partnership may be initiated by low-income communities or supporting NGOs by approaching (lobbying or pressuring) local government to constitute a partnership embracing the appropriate authorities and agencies and providing the necessary managerial supports and capacity building that may be required to ensure its efficacy, operational efficiency and sustainability.

While the term 'partnership' has been in common usage to denote the participation of the formal private sector, and occasionally urban poor communities and NGOs, with government authorities and agencies in public-private partnerships (PPPs), for the development and management of public housing projects and programmes since the 1980s, few have been authentic partnerships. Most often the term 'partnership' has been attached to conventional contracting and subcontracting arrangements for the implementation of government-initiated and controlled projects and, most commonly, the procurement and management of 'public' infrastructure and delivery of services, notably water, waste, energy and transport. By contrast, in the United Kingdom, for example, the NGO National Custom and Self Build Association (NaCSBA) provides advice and negotiating assistance and training to individuals and groups in forming partnerships with local government authorities for the self-building of new urban housing[16] (Broome 2007). Rarely, if ever, have they been authentic partnerships founded on mutualism, interdependence, respect and trust (Fowler 1998).

These values underpinned the very effective 'authentic' partnership in Mumbai, India, that engaged the State of Maharashtra Slum Rehabilitation Authority (SRA), the Indian National Slum Dwellers Federation (NSDF), Mahila Milan, a local community-based organisation, and SPARC (Society for the Promotion of Area Resource Centres), a Mumbai-based NGO. Through shared values of mutual understanding and respect and prolonged negotiations, in the mid-1990s the partnership was able to employ state legislation for the application of transferrable development rights (TDRs), administered by the SRA, to acquire well-located land and develop it with fully serviced, affordable housing for the resettlement of some 900 families who had previously lived in precarious un-serviced squatter slums on railway trackside-reservation land in extreme danger, particularly to children, from fast-moving trains (Burra 1999).

Partnerships as economic means and social-developmental ends

Well-working partnerships are a means to ensure efficient and sustainable production and management of housing and urban development. As an end, they build social capital in low-income group communities and can strengthen local-level democracy and the inclusion of 'marginalised' households and communities in the wider society, economy and fabric of the city (Geddes 2000).

As a means to the efficient, effective and equitable production and management of urban housing, partnerships can draw on the collective and cooperative knowledge, experience, skills, understanding and financial resources of all partners, thereby avoiding much of the misunderstanding and subsequent conflicts between the producers and consumers of housing that have tended to typify public housing projects (Abbott 1996). The confidence generated by the participatory engagement of low-income group partners in all stages of the housing production processes can release substantial household monetary wealth (from savings and informal loans), obviating the need for extensive financial subsidies. For instance, evidence from Kenya, Sri Lanka and Senegal shows that, with appropriate financial and social security, even very low-income households can and will invest several times the value of government inputs in the construction or improvement of their dwellings and neighbourhood environment in addition to contributing their human energy and skills (Wakely 2018, p.107).

Engaging low-income group representatives (community leaders) with government decision-makers (politicians), managers and technical professionals in ways that expose each to the values, ambitions and constraints faced by each other generates an understanding and sense of solidarity in the face of specific problems or possible courses of action, maximising, if not ensuring, the achievement of jointly agreed goals.

Furthermore, as an end, the responsibility of recognised membership of an official decision-making body engenders the development and/or strengthening of sustainable democratic governance and managerial processes within neighbourhood communities, such as the appointing/electing of leaders/representative members of partnership bodies, committees, etc., which invariably require skill and management training and other capacity-building inputs that go beyond the confines of housing production and local environmental development (Nelson & Wright 1995).

The values of mutualism, interdependence, respect and trust, required for the foundation of authentic partnerships, are rarely, if ever, spontaneously shared by potential partners in the production, maintenance and management of low-income group urban housing. Local (municipal) government and local-level branches of national housing authorities and utility agencies tend to have different objectives and operational styles that frequently lead to antagonism and competition between them. In any city it is common for the residents of urban low-income settlements to embrace a wide range of household groups, perhaps with different ethnic origins, with distinct customs, beliefs and aspirations, in competition, even conflict, between them. So the essential starting point of any partnership arrangement that leads to unity is a process of learning and communication with the aim of engendering understanding and a consensus based on respect and trust—a difficult but rewarding process, referred to by Mackintosh (1992) as a process of transformation in which all partners accept a need for changes of perceptions and relationships and demonstrate a willingness to learn.

Hitherto in this account, emphasis has been given to project-level partnerships for the planning and implementation of specific interventions engaging particular neighbourhoods and low-income group communities, embracing both relatively short-term activities, such as the location, planning, design and supervision of new housing and urban development interventions, and longer-term engagement in the routine management and maintenance of public and social housing,[17] infrastructure and services.

The principles and strategic operation of authentic, inclusive partnership can also be employed beneficially for metropolitan and regional levels of decision-making. For example, under the Sri Lanka 'Million Houses Programme' 1982–89, Housing and Community Development Committees (HCDCs) were established in each of the country's 25 administrative districts to determine policy and implementation strategies for urban social housing production, maintenance and management. The HCDCs were partnerships, chaired by the District Secretary (chief executive of local government administration), that included representation of all relevant district authorities and national government line ministries and agencies, as well as active NGOs and representation of urban low-income group organisations. In 1996 in Kenya, the Nairobi Informal Settlements Coordination Committee (NISCC) was established as a partnership embracing the political and administrative leadership of Nairobi province and city, their technical officers, city-based NGOs and representatives of community organisations of the city's 134 informal settlements to collaboratively set the criteria and establish priorities for the implementation of a national 'Local Authority Service Delivery Action Plan' (LASDAP), a Government of Kenya poverty-reduction programme, based on the principles of local participatory budgeting. This partnership was particularly successful in bringing together the hitherto widely divergent political antagonism between the provincial and city administrations in embracing the priorities of the urban poor residents for investment in infrastructure in informal settlements. In 2000, the (Labour) government of the United Kingdom enacted a policy to encourage and provide support for local government councils to establish and operate so-called 'arms-length management organisations'(ALMOs) as partnerships[18] that embraced public housing estate tenants, local government councillors and technical officers, and some council-appointed (NGO) members to manage all public housing. A decade later (by 2010), more than half the public housing in the United Kingdom (over a million dwellings across 65 of the c.420 local government housing authorities in the UK) were managed by ALMOs with names such as Wolverhampton Homes; Hackney Homes (London) and Nottingham City Homes (Boughton 2018).

Authentic local government and community partnerships for the production and management of urban low-income group housing are, of essence, politically non-partisan, though with strong social-democratic ideals. However, with good understanding, their egalitarian operational principles that disallow dominance by any particular member (group) open them to members of any reasonably conducive political persuasion. However, if partnership is to be more meaningful than token 'box-ticking', there is a need for a determined political will by governments to engage constructively with organisations of the urban poor, which, in many countries and cities, demands significant political change.

Notes

1 Through an Oxfam-supported project by women and young people in the village of Arabsolangi in Sindh, India.
2 This group was the embryonic start to what ultimately became the 'Lewisham Self-Build Housing Association' that functions in subsequent developments in Lewisham and neighbouring boroughs in south east London, carried out by the 'South London Family Housing Association'.
3 Walter Segal was a German-born British Architect, with strong social and environmental concerns in favour of engaging households and communities

in all stages of the design and construction of their own dwellings, had already developed a flexible, adjustable system of timber-frame-based house construction, using only hand-tools, suitable for construction by untrained DIY-builders and for the topographical conditions of mature tree-covered uneven and steeply-sloping building sites—ideal for the first Lewisham self-build projects.

Walter Segal died in 1985; so, the second and subsequent projects, using his system were supervised by Jon Broome, who had worked closely with Walter on the initial project (Grahamme & McKean 2021).

4 Segal's task was facilitated by his friendship with Brian Richardson, with whom he shared anarchist political leanings! (Broome & Richardson 1995, p.74).

5 Walter Segal's structural-timber-based system was not a 'kit of parts', but a design using affordable standard materials and components readily available on the retail building materials market (e.g. timber in standard lengths in order to minimise cutting and wastage).

6 Much of the commentary on the 'Lewisham Self-Build Housing' venture has been in architectural profession journals that tend to focus more on the technical and design techniques of Walter Segal's building system than on the policy and administrative innovations that it brought to the Borough's public social housing programme (Ellis 1989/2019)

7 Lewisham Borough Planning, Architect's, Engineer's, District Surveyor's Departments; the Borough Treasurer's, Valuer's, and Solicitor's Departments; etc.

8 GLC Planning and Regeneration Committee, London Fire Brigade; the Department (Ministry) for the Environment (DOE); the National Federation of Housing Associations.

9 Remembering the frustration of pre-work -on-site in the first project, sketch designs for alternative house types were prepared prior to discussions with potential self-builders about their housing needs and aspirations, thereby shifting the options slightly more to a conventional, architect-led public housing procurement process, though the flexibility of the Segal system that facilitated design variations, annulled the appearance of any such regressive change of emphasis. Subsequently, all the houses in the second project in Honor Oak have were extended and altered by their occupants so that they all look very different from each other.

10 London SE13 7UU

11 The occupants' participation was principally confined to the fit-out of individual flats and maisonettes and communal facilities including the installation of non-load-bearing internal walls, and kitchens and bathrooms, plumbing, wiring and ventilation systems and more generally to decorations and landscaping and planting of the external areas of the project site.

12 In the 1980s the privatisation of many hitherto public services and facilities was strongly promoted by the World Bank and other multi-lateral development agencies under the rubric of 'structural adjustment programmes' (SAPs) of economic and administrative reform, in the belief that the 'enterprise culture' of the profit-motivated private sector ensures efficacy and efficiency.

34 *Implementation strategies*

13 See: the seminal publications: Abrams, C. 1964, *"Housing in the Modern World: Man's Struggle for Shelter in an Urbanising World"*, MIT Press, Cambridge MA USA; and Turner, J.F.C. & R.Fichter (eds) 1972, *"Freedom to Build: Dweller Control of the Housing Process"*, Macmillan, New York, USA.
14 The 'Model Cities Program' (1966–69) was initiated in and administered by the Federal Department of Housing and Urban Development (HUD) as a political reaction to the urban riots in several American cities in the mid 1960s.
15 Detractors might say 'compromise' (Wassenhoven 2022, pp.351–386)
16 See: https://nacsba.org.uk
17 A distinction is made between: 1) public rental housing, owned by the (local) state; and 2) social housing that is (constructed), owned and managed by low-income households and/or community-based institutions (Wakely 2018, pp.88, 99).
18 Asbos are regarded legally as 'wholly owned local authority non-profit companies', though there are political suspicions of their becoming but thinly-disguised vehicles for the commercial privatisation of public rental housing (with substantial profits accruing to private shareholders).

References

Abbott, J. 1996 *'Sharing the city: Community participation in urban management'*, Earthscan, London, UK.
Alimuddin, S., A. Hasan & A. Sadiq 2004 *'The work of the Anjuman Samaji Behbood in Faisalabad, Pakistan'*, in Mitlin, D. & D. Satterthwaite (eds) 'Empowering squatter citizen: Local government, civil society and urban poverty reduction', Earthscan, London, UK.
Alkire, S. 2004. *'Valuing freedoms: Sen's capability approach and poverty reduction'*, Chapter 7, in 'Valuing freedoms: Sen's capability approach and poverty reduction', Oxford Scholarship e-edition.
Birchall, J. 1988 *'Building communities the co-operative way'*, Routledge & Kegan Paul, London, UK.
Boughton, J. 2018 *'Municipal dreams: The rise and fall of council housing'*, Verso, London, UK.
Broome, J. & B. Richardson 1995 *'The self-build book: How to enjoy designing and building your own home'*, Green Books Ltd, Cambridge, UK.
Burra, S. 1999 *'Resettlement and rehabilitation of the urban poor: The story of Kanjur Marg'*, DPU Working Paper No.99, UCL, London, UK.
Cheema, S. 1991 *'Cities, people & poverty: Urban development cooperation for the 1990s'*, UNDP Strategy Paper, UNDP, New York, USA.
Das, P. 2015 *'The urban sanitation conundrum: What can community managed programmes in India Unravel'*, Environment & Urbanization, Vol.27, No.2, Sage, London, UK.
Davidson, J., D. Myers, & M. Chakraborty 1992 *'No time to waste'*, Oxfam, Oxford, UK.
Ellis, C. 1987 (digital re-issue 2019) *'Walter's way, self-build schemes in Lewisham, London by the Segal method'*, Architectural Review, London, UK, https://lewisham.gov.uk/myservices/planning/policy/self-build-and-custom-build-homes (accessed Jun.2023)

E&U 2011 '*Community-driven disaster risk reduction and climate change adaptation in urban areas*', Environment & Urbanization, Vol.23, No.2, Sage, London, UK (Journal issue of 14 individually-authored papers).

Frediani, A. 2007 '*Amartya Sen, the World Bank and the redress of urban poverty: A Brazilian case study*', Journal of Human Development, Vol.8, No.1, Routledge, Abingdon, UK.

Geddes, M. 2000 '*Tackling social inclusion in the European Union: The limits to the new orthodoxy of local partnership*', International Journal of Urban and Regional Research, Vol.24, No.4, Wiley, London, UK.

Gibson, T. 1979 '*People power: Community and works groups in action*', Pelican, London, UK.

Grahamme, A. & J. McKean 2021 '*Walter Segal, self-built architect*', Lund Humphries, London, UK.

Hague, C., P. Wakely, J. Crespin, & C. Jasko 2006 '*Making planning work: A guide to approaches and skills*' (pp.43–45), ITDG Publishing, Rugby, UK.

Hamdi, N. & R. Goethert 1997 '*Action planning for cities: A guide to community practice*', John Ailey & Sons, Chichester, UK.

Hastings, A. 1996 '*Unravelling the process of partnership in urban regeneration policy*', Urban Studies, Vol.33, No.2, Sage, London, UK.

Helming, S. & M. Göbel 1997 '*ZOPP: Objectives-oriented project planning*', GTZ, Frankfurt, Germany.

Kämpchen, M. 2013 '*Precarious balance*', in 'D+C development cooperation e-newsletter', https://www.dandc.eu/en/article/poverty-more-mere-lack-material-goods (accessed Jun.2020).

Mackintosh, M. 1992 '*Partnership: Issues of policy and negotiation*', Local Economy, Vol.7, Sage, London, UK.

Mayo, S. 1993 '*Housing: Enabling markets to work*', World Bank Policy Paper, World Bank, Washington, DC, USA.

Mitlin, D. 2008a '*Urban poor funds: Development by the people for the people*', IIED Poverty Reduction in Urban Areas Working Paper 18, IIED, London.

Nelson, N. & S. Wright (eds) 1995 '*Power and participatory development: Theory and practice*', ITDG Publishing, Rugby, UK.

Sen, A. 1985 '*Commodities and capabilities*', Oxford University Press, New York.

Wakely, P. 2018 '*Housing in developing cities: Experience & lessons*', Routledge/Taylor and Francis, New York, USA and Abingdon, UK

Wakely, P. 2020 '*Partnership: A strategic paradigm for the production and management of affordable housing and sustainable urban development*', International Journal of Urban Sustainable Development, Vol.12, No.1, Taylor & Francis, Abingdon, UK.

Wakely, P. & S. Matararachchi 2021 '*Sustainable community governance and management of urban housing and local environment*', Town Planning Review, Vol. 92, No. 4, Liverpool University Press, Liverpool, UK.

Wilkinson, A. 2020 '*Local response in health emergencies: Key considerations for addressing the COVID-19 pandemic in informal urban Settlements*', Environment & Urbanization, Vol.32, No.2, Sage, London, UK.

3   Land and location

Urban households and communities will only invest their energy and resources in their dwellings and workplaces if they have absolute confidence in the security of their rights to the land, which they develop with service infrastructure and on which they construct their houses and neighbourhood facilities. Thus, legally recognised security of tenure or title[1] to land ranks amongst the most fundamental supports needed to enable the development of safe and socially acceptable urban housing. Secure and acceptable tenure or title deeds may take one, or several, of a range of statutory and/or 'customary' forms, even combined within the same urban housing neighbourhood, programme or project—even property (Payne 2022, pp.205–221).

3.1 Location

Much of the discussion on participation and partnerships in Chapters 1 and 2 is directed to the upgrading and improvement of existing substandard (informal) urban neighbourhoods by/with the households and communities that they accommodate; thus, their location has already been determined. Whether or not they are officially/formally recognised, they are already part of the urban fabric and housing stock.

Determining the location of new housing for/by urban low-income households is of fundamental importance to its future occupants and users (Phe & Wakely2000) and to the structure (urban form) of the whole town or city of which they are an integral part (Landry 2006 pp.19–29). Hitherto, the location of land for low-income group housing by municipal development and planning authorities has been largely determined by the capital costs of its procurement and development: notably, the price of land; cost of its development with trunk infrastructure or off-plot linkages to existing infrastructure networks. In many instances, this has led to untenable social and economic disruption, leading to the failure/abandonment of new housing projects (Wakely 2018, pp.120–123). A major determinant of this category of locational problems has been the high value of available urban land, reducing

DOI: 10.4324/9781003465546-3

options to the acquisition and development of peri-urban land on the fringes of towns and cities, far from infrastructure, service and social networks, and from centres of accessible employment for people typically with few marketable urban skills and ability to afford the cost of transport (if it exists at all) to more central places, where such opportunities are likely to be located. For example, an evaluation of the Inter-American Development Bank (IDB)-supported Low-Income Settlements Programme (LISP) in Guyana in the 1990s reported that

[many project sites were] distant from existing infrastructure and services leading to low occupation rates due to affordability issues (people could not afford to build houses) and to infrastructure and service deficiencies. Sites were in distant locations where transport costs were too high. Because of the high cost of extending trunk infrastructure to the site, support services such as schools, clinics and playing fields were planned for but not built. There was no commerce on site and no nearby employment.

(Gattoni 2009)

Similar observations were made about the Fundación Salvadoreña de Desarollo y Vivienda Mínima (FSDVM)-led housing programme in El Salvador and elsewhere (Van der Linden 1992, pp.341–353). New ethical values and long-term foresight emerging from recent concerns in the wake of greater and more widespread understanding of the implications of global heating and the existential risks of pathogenic transmissions from the lessons learned from the 2020–23 COVID-19 pandemic are likely to question validity of the prevailing economic and financial values. Inevitably, such measures will incur higher capital costs of off-plot infrastructure works and house construction than in the past, for which many households will not be able or willing to pay. Full infrastructure costs may therefore have to be subsidised by the relevant public sector agencies, and, as it is unlikely that standards of space within dwellings will be able to be governed by building-control legislation, health considerations, such as viral infections within households, should constitute a significant component of participatory support-education in urban housing development processes (Wakely & Matararachchi 2021). So ubiquitous have been the hazards and risks incurred by coronavirus that they will live on in urban and rural 'folklore', even of generations that did not experience the pandemic, as have those of preceding plagues, epidemics and recurrent geophysical disasters, thus becoming accepted as commonsense practice in the planning, management and financing of dwellings and neighbourhoods.

Urban households and communities will only invest their energy and resources in their dwellings and workplaces if they have absolute confidence in the security of their rights to the land, which they develop with service infrastructure and construct their houses and neighbourhood facilities. Thus, legally recognised security of tenure or title to land ranks amongst the most fundamental supports needed to enable the development of safe and socially acceptable urban housing. Secure and acceptable tenure or title deeds may take one, or several, of a range of statutory and/or 'customary' forms, even combined within the same urban housing neighbourhood, programme or project—even the same property (Payne 2022, pp.205–221).

The bottom line in determining the location of new low-income housing provision (projects) in towns and cities rests not only on the capital cost of its acquisition and development and their impacts on the wider urban environment and economy but, more importantly, on the social and economic needs and aspirations of their future residents and users; hence the importance of their engagement in the initial (citywide) decision-making processes.

3.2 Geophysical determinants

Geophysical conditions are a significant determinant in identifying appropriate land for low-income group housing. On occasion these have included undeveloped land that is structurally unstable due to natural or human-made topographical conditions, such as the neighbourhood of Tal al Zarazier in Aleppo, Syria, built on un-compacted landfill over a former solid waste dump with a natural subterranean stream/surface-water drain running through it, or land that is prone to periodic or unpredictable inundation.

Urban households and communities will only invest their energy and resources in their dwellings and workplaces if they have absolute confidence in the security of their rights to the land, which they develop with service infrastructure and construct their houses and neighbourhood facilities. Thus, legally recognised security of tenure or title to land ranks amongst the most fundamental supports needed to enable the development of safe and socially acceptable urban housing. Secure and acceptable tenure or title deeds may take one, or several, of a range of statutory and/or 'customary' forms, even combined within the same urban housing neighbourhood, programme or project—even the same property. (Payne 2022, pp.205–221).

The bottom line in determining the location of new low-income housing provision (projects) in towns and cities rests not only on the capital cost of its acquisition and development and their impacts on the wider urban environment and economy, but, more importantly, on the social and economic needs and aspirations of their future residents and users; hence the importance of their engagement in the initial (citywide) decision-making processes.

Coastal locations

For historical political/economic reasons, a large proportion of the world's towns and cities are in coastal locations, exposed to climatically generated hazards.[2] It is estimated that over 70 percent of the world's urban population live and work in towns and cities in 'low-level' coastal locations, subject to tidal surges, storms, cyclones, hurricanes and tsunamis caused by distant seabed seismic eruptions and long-term changes in mean sea level, generated by a rise in mean global seawater temperatures and the melting of the Arctic and Antarctic ice caps due to global heating (UN-Habitat 2011, p.4). Many large-scale projects have been implemented in attempts to minimise the flooding of coastal towns and cities that include low-lying land, fit for housing and other

Figure 3.1 Hong Kong vertical-type sea wall
(Photo: CEDD, HK SAR, 2019)

developments. These range from heavy engineering examples such as the Hong Kong Sea Defence system of more than 50 km. of heavy concrete and granite sea walls[3] surrounding Hong Kong Island, Kowloon and Tsing Yi within Victoria Harbour (TFWL 2015).

Also the Thames Barrier, a complex construction of sluice gates, across the river in the east of the city of London, constructed in the 1970s, that, when

Figure 3.2 Thames Barrier in the process of raising the sluice gates
(Photo: Andy Roberts/Wikipedia, 2004)

lowered, allow for the passage of seagoing shipping[4] and, in anticipation of storms and high sea surges, can be raised, impounding water in the river's estuary on the downstream side of the barrier,[5] in order to prevent flooding in the centre of London. However, by the 2000s, only 30 years after its construction at a cost of over £5.3million, it was estimated that the rise in global sea level had rendered the Barrier inadequate, even when fully raised.

A simpler, more reliable and better-tested approach to mitigating coastal flooding, and erosion in towns and cities, is the management of vegetation, notably, where possible, mangroves that not only stem the force of tidal and sea-current surges onto the land and bind the coastal front against erosion but are also highly effective absorbers of CO_2 and breeding grounds for coastal fauna. In India, the Maharashtra State Mangrove Protection and Monitoring Committee, with support from the Union Government, is responsible for conserving and maintaining mangrove swamps that protect the western coasts of Mumbai at Mahim Bay and Navi Mumbai, on the Kolkan coast, from the devastation of flooding in the cities, such as that in Mumbai in 2005 (DasGupta & Shaw 2013).[6]

Notes

1 See Chapter 4 later.
2 E.g. The flood in Mumbai, India in 2005, occasioned by excessive rainfall (>1,200 mm in 24 hrs) and tidal surges in the Arabian Sea, accounted for

Figure 3.3 Coastal mangroves
(Photo: Santiago Moreno, 2022)

over 1,000 deaths by drowning and rendering thousands of low-income families homeless, caused extensive flooding throughout the city, notably, over low-lying land in the Northern suburbs, part of which was destined for the construction, *inter alia*, of low-income group housing.

3 There are two types of sea wall: vertical walls (see Fig.3. + (TFWL 2015, p.9), and sloping sea defences that included ingenious artificially formed habitats to nurture the diversity of local inter-tidal marine fauna and flora; parts of the vertical-type wall also incorporate less elaborate ecological habitats, for small species. Nevertheless, unsubstantiated observations have been made that the wall has exacerbated the pollution within Victoria Harbour.

4 Access to the former Port of London had ceased to function in its inner-city stretch of the river by the 1970s, as docks opened out of the city downstream, in the Thames estuary, in order to be able to handle larger vessels, the increase of tonnage of cargo and containerisation.

5 Entailing: shoring up and maintaining the riverfront and jetties of the largely industrial areas of South Barking and Dagenham on the North bank; and developing the recreational waterway network of lakes and canals to take up excess flood water in the residential neighbourhoods of Thamesmead and North Plumstead on the South bank of the river, close to the barrier.

6 E.g. The 2005 flood in Mumbai, (see Note 2 earlier).

References

DasGupta, R. & R. Shaw 2013 '*Changing perspectives of mangrove management in India*', Ocean and Coastal Management, Vol.80, Elsevier, Amsterdam, Netherlands.

Gattoni, G. (2009) '*A case for the incremental housing in sites-and-services programs*', paper presented at IDB conference, http://idbdocs.iadb.org/WSDocs/getDocument.aspx?DOCNUM-2062811 (accessed Nov.2022)

Landry, C. 2006 '*The art of city making*', Earthscan, London, UK.

Payne, G. 2020 '*Land, rights & innovation: Improving tenure security for the urban poor*', ITDG Publishing, Rugby, UK.

Payne, G. 2022 '*Somewhere to live: Rising to the global urban land and housing challenge*', Practical Action Publishing Ltd, Rugby, UK.

Phe, H.H. & P. Wakely 2000 '*Status, quality and the other trade-off: Towards a new theory of urban residential location*', Urban Studies, Vol.37, No.1, Glasgow, UK.

Schwaab, J. 2021 '*Trees cool the land surface temperature of cities by up to 12°C*', New Scientist, No.3361, London, UK.

TFWL 2015 '*Functions and design considerations of Sea Wall*', Civil Engineering Division, Government of Hong Kong Special Administrative Region, Hong Kong, https://www.hfc.org.hk/filemanager/files/TFWL_02_2015.pdf (accessed Feb.2023).

UN-Habitat 2011 '*Cities and climate change' global report on human settlements 2011*', Earthscan, London, UK.

Van der Linden, J. 1992 '*Back to the roots: Keys to successful implementation of sites-and-services*', in Mathéy, K. (ed) 'Beyond self-help housing', Mansell Publishing, London, UK.

Wakely, P. 2018 '*Housing in developing cities: Experience and lessons*', Routledge, Taylor and Francis, New York, USA & London, UK.

4 Land use and landscape planning and management

Customarily, land use planning of housing areas, even for the development of sites and services projects in which house plot allotees have been individually responsible for their own plot development and dwelling construction, has been undertaken centrally by local authority urban planners and designers. Where cooperative partnerships, embracing prospective occupier-communities, as described in Chapter 2, have been established, they will be able to have a significant role in the neighbourhood planning process. This was well demonstrated in the Zambia Squatter Upgrading Programme in Lusaka in the 1970s in which, for example, households occupying dwellings or neighbourhoods that could not economically be upgraded with infrastructure were voluntarily grouped in neighbourhood subgroups of 25 households, each of which would share a communal sanitary facility[1] in a new sites-and-services scheme located close to their original informal (shanty) dwellings. Each community subgroup, working together with Lusaka City Council urban planners, was responsible for planning the layout of roads, the location of their sanitary facilities and the distribution of individual house plots within its designated area in the sites and services project area (Jere 1984, pp.55–68). A similar example of the engagement of a low-income group community working in partnership with local government agencies on the land use planning and property tenure rights was the West Green Place improvement and extension project in the London Borough of Harringay in the 1970s, initiated and managed by the architects Hunt Thompson Associates (HTA 2022).

Local government administrations in towns and cities in regions prone to climate change-induced and other geophysical hazards, such as earthquakes, landslides, coastal storms/cyclones and tsunamis, are generally aware of the risks of potential disaster and, in most cases, include mitigation measures in their planning and building procedures and legislation (World Bank 2015). However, urban low-income group housing areas and informal settlements are frequently not protected by such official safety measures, as they are regarded as 'illegal', rendering them the most prone to such disasters. In these situations, therefore, there is a need to ensure that appropriate precautions are taken

DOI: 10.4324/9781003465546-4

in the location and planning of areas designated for low-income group housing development, and that appropriate advice and technical support is given
to the design and construction of dwellings and community buildings, also to
the provision of such measures as safe escape routes and robust buildings of
permanent construction such as community centres and schools that can act as
storm shelters in the case of flooding by surge tides, tsunamis and cyclones in
coastal towns and cities.

4.1 Local land planning and management

Invariably, the distribution of land uses of urban low-income group housing
areas has been based on maximising its economic efficiency and financial
returns, leading to the highest possible residential densities and 'productivity'
of land allocated for private use[2]—'The higher the better'!– reducing the ratio
of 'unproductive' land necessary for local public services and amenities to the
barest minimum. In the vast Arumbakkam sites-and-services project in Chennai, India, initiated in the 1970s by the then Madras Metropolitan Development
Authority (MMDA) with a World Bank loan to the Tamil Nadu (State) Housing Board, of the 32.3-hectare project site, 46 percent (15has) was devoted to
housing plots and 25 percent (8has) for roads and access ways; the remaining
30 percent of the site was allocated to formal commercial and industrial development, providing some local employment opportunities, and to institutional
buildings, including schools and health facilities, and one small community
hall, serving a total population of some 11,000.[3] No public land was provided
for communal landscaped open-air social or recreational activities (Swan et al.
1983, pp.100–118).

4.2 Participation and partnerships in land use planning and maintenance

As noted earlier, urban low-income group housing areas and informal settlements are frequently not protected by official safety measures,[4] as they are
regarded as 'illegal', rendering them the most prone to disasters. In these situations, therefore, there is a need to ensure that appropriate precautions are taken
in the location and planning of areas designated for low-income group incremental housing development, and that appropriate advice and technical support
is given to the design and construction of dwellings and community buildings,
also to the provision of such measures as safe escape routes and robust buildings of permanent construction such as community centres and schools that
can act as storm shelters in the case of flooding by surge tides, tsunamis and
cyclones in coastal towns and cities. It is important that such measures are
designed and implemented by local authorities in close collaboration, or partnership, with the communities that are in potential danger; also that reliable

communication and early-warning procedures are in place and well understood and rehearsed.

In the immediate wake of the 2004 Asian tsunami, the government of Sri Lanka declared all land within 100–200 metres from the mean high water-line an interim nationwide coastal 'buffer zone', in which it was prohibited to construct or repair any buildings, regardless of its coastline topography or whether it was urban or rural. The interim buffer zone served the purpose of obviating any *ad hoc* opportunistic, land-grabbing and unauthorised (unsafe) development in the inevitably chaotic immediate aftermath of the tragedy, but soon had to be replaced by a more locally specific set of development control measures that also embraced the ecological conservation of the fragile natural coastal environment. In urban areas, new environmental safety measures were drawn up by local authorities, such as Galle Municipal Council, in conjunction with the national Urban Development Authority (UDA) and the participation of local private sector institutions, NGOs and CBOs. These were then incorporated in the relevant planning and building by-laws, governing all seafront development, including low-income group housing and enterprises, mostly occupied by fishermen and other sea-dependent trades.

The lessons learnt from the Sri Lankan example for the mitigation of risk from coastal threats apply equally to other geophysical hazards and those originating from extreme climatic occurrences, induced by global climate change, such as riparian flooding caused by storms, hurricanes and cyclones or glacial meltwater from unusually high temperatures in mountainous regions that may be a considerable distance from the urban area of impact. Such occurrences are not uncommon in parts of the Andes in South America. As well as causing hazards from surface run-off, flooding resulting from heavy and persistent rainfall can cause groundwater saturation that can precipitate landslides in steeply inclined topography, which, in many cities, are the only sites of informal settlements where the lowest-income group households can afford to live and work.

Pathogen-safe communal open spaces

Reference has already been made to the need for adequate open space, with particular regard to facilitating safe social interaction, community governance and recreation, in the context of 'social distancing' to minimise the risk of the transmission of viral pathogens.

In addition, there is a strong case to be made for providing land and managerial support for community-based subsistence and market horticultural production,[5] particularly in those Sub-Saharan African cities, in which many low-income group immigrant households maintain close and frequent contact with their villages-of-origin, from which they receive basic foodstuff that may be disrupted due to climate change hazards or unaffordable increases in transport costs.

Figure 4.1 Pablo VI-2 Bogotá, Colombia: Small meeting area and basketball court behind, managed and maintained by the neighbourhood CBO 'La Administración'

(Photo: Luz Stella Echeverri, 2023)

Figure 4.2 Andarai, Rio de Janeiro, Brazil: Five-a-side football pitch constructed in high-density favela, as part of the Favela Bairro upgrading programme (Wakely 2018, pp.68–74)—n.b: trees in background, nurtured in public places and access ways by local neighbourhood residents' associations

(Photo: Patrick Wakely, 2010)

Figure 4.3 Oshakati, Namibia: Squatter settlement community hall and meeting ground, under construction by community volunteers. (n.b: trees on house plots, in background, nurtured by households' wastewater, as a condition of OHSIP upgrading project (Wakely 2018, pp.74–78)

(Photo: Gitte Jacobsen, 1995)

Figure 4.4 London, UK: Hilldrop Housing Estate, trees and planting maintained by London Borough of Islington in collaboration with Hilldrop Area Community Association. Hilldrop Community Centre in background

(Photo: Patrick Wakely, 2023)

Appropriate support to such community cultivation[6] (small plots of cultivatable land, similar to urban allotments in UK[7]) also helps reinforce community social development and cohesion. As well, they enhance ambient CO_2 absorption capacity, in addition to the planting and maintenance of shade trees and other maintainable grass-covered open spaces, as discussed in Chapter 3.

Figure 4.5 Malakal, South Sudan: Shade trees planted in the public market by the community market traders to provide shade and protection against desert sandstorms; they also absorb CO_2

(Photo: Patrick Wakely, 2006)

Figure 4.6 Oxford, UK: Suburban 'allotments'

(Photo: Rachel Hamdi, 2023)

The land use planning of new housing neighbourhoods has generally been undertaken by local government professionals or, in the case of private sector developments, planning consultants, who are rarely, if ever, able to engage with the future occupants and users of their planning schemes. Therefore, they can only draw on their professional training and personal experience and that of those who precede them, and on prevailing official planning standards, guidelines, by-laws and development controls. However, examples exist of self-build urban housing projects in the Global North (Broome 2007) and South (Wakely 2018, pp.134–136) alike, where the communities of aspiring self-builders and resettled future occupants and users have collaborated, or joined in partnerships with local authorities in the planning of their new neighbourhoods. But the overriding tendency remains that of the distribution and layout of individual private plots, rather than the urban design and landscaping of the communal land between them, maximising the former and giving less attention to the shared local environment.[8] The 2021–23 COVID-19 pandemic drew attention to 'social distancing' and the need for people to be able to communicate and socialise safely in outdoor conditions in which pathogenic transfers are minimised, occasioning lower gross residential densities than those determined by the prevailing values of economic and financial efficiency, as outlined earlier.

In addition to environmental health considerations, increased areas of public open space and neighbourhood facilities are required to allow for community recreation and casual social interaction between otherwise housebound people, notably women, also local sports facilities to foster mental health and social conviviality, particularly of young adults and children; also to provide larger gathering spaces to enable events related to communal activities such as collective community governance. As a contribution to global heating, where climatically and topographically possible, the planting and nurture of trees and other CO_2-absorbing vegetation needs to be encouraged and supported. For example, funding and technical support to the upgrading of dwellings and services in the Oshakati Human Settlements Improvement Programme in Namibia was conditional on the planting and nurture of shade trees on each upgraded plot in low-income group housing areas as a social/climatic amenity and to lower the ambient air temperature and stabilise the desertic soil, which, coincidentally, also increased the safe capture of CO_2, thereby contributing to the local amelioration of global heating[9] on the fringes of the Kalahari Desert (Wakely 2018, pp.74–83).

Inevitably, measures to overcome such conditions will incur relatively high capital costs of off-plot infrastructure works and house construction, for which many households will not be able or willing to pay. Full infrastructure costs may therefore have to be subsidised by the relevant public sector agencies and, as it is unlikely that standards of space within dwellings will be able to be governed by building-control legislation, health considerations, such as viral infections within households, should constitute a significant component of participatory support-education in urban housing development processes

(Wakely & Matararachchi 2021). So ubiquitous have been the hazards and risks incurred by the coronavirus pandemic of 2021–23 that they will probably live on in urban and rural 'folklore', even of generations that did not experience the pandemic, as have those of preceding plagues, epidemics and recurrent geophysical disasters, thus becoming accepted as common-sense practice in the planning, management and financing of dwellings and neighbourhoods.

In summary, conscientious urban design and landscaping[10] is central to the social need and use of communal open space in urban low-income housing areas and is of prime importance to both the mitigation of pathogenic transmission and the reduction of 'greenhouse gas' emissions. With care in the induction stages of establishing community organisations/partnerships, as discussed in Chapter 2, the value of communal open-air neighbourhood facilities and its husbandry becomes widely accepted by the leaders and membership of neighbourhood-based CBOs, as evidenced by the many examples referred to in the preceding chapters.

Notes

1 Potable waterpoint, washing, bathing and toilet facilities.
2 Usually termed 'plot ratio' (i.e. ratio of private land area to total land area in a residential neighbourhood or housing estate).
3 Gross residential density = >330 persons/ha.
4 Development control laws
5 The Nairobi and Environs Food Security, Agriculture and Landscape Forum (NEFSALF) was established in Nairobi, Kenya, in 2002, as a network for the exchange of information, skill and marketing training for urban small-scale agricultural producers, in the city (Mazingira 2022)
6 Managerial and marketing advice, provision of basic horticultural tools, insurance, etc.
7 Also, 'The National Victory Garden Program', established by the Federal Government in USA in the depression years of the 1930s.
8 For which the urban planning educator, Leslie Ginsburg, coined the cynical acronym SLOAP (Space Left Over After Planning)!
9 The cooling effect of trees comes largely from shading and transpiration, which is when water within the tree is released as vapour through the leaves. This process takes heat energy from the surrounding environment by evaporation, lowering the ambient air temperature (Schwaab 2021).
10 that includes CO_2-absorbing planting (trees, shrubs, grass, etc).

References

Broome, J. 2007, '*The Green Self-Build Book*', Green Books Ltd, Cambridge, UK.
Conaty, P. & M. Large 2013, "*Commons Sense: Co-Operative Place Making and the Capturing of Land Value*", 21st Century Garden Cities, Manchester, UK.

HTA. 2022, '*Altered Estates: How to reconcile competing interests in estate regeneration*' HTA Design, London, UK, www.alteredestates.co.uk (accessed Dec.2022)

Jere, H. 1984 "*Lusaka: Local Participation in Planning and Decision-making*" in Payne, G. (ed) 'Low Income Housing in the Developing World: the Role of Sites and Services and Settlement Upgrading', Wiley, Chichester, UK.

Lewis, M. & P. Conaty, 2012 "*The Reliance Imperative: Cooperative Transitions to a Steady State Economy*", New Society, Gabriola Island, BC, Canada.

Max Locke Centre 2005, "*The Rough Guide to Community Asset Management*" MLC Press, University of Westminster, London, UK.

Mazingira Institute 2002, "*Mazingira Newsletter, Issue 1*", Mazingira Institute, Nairobi, Kenya. https://mazinst.org/ (accessed May 2023)

Madden, D. & P. Marcuse 2016 '*In Defense of Housing*', Verso, London, UK.

McAuslan, P. 2002 '*Tenure and the law: the Legality of illegality and the illegality of legality*', chapter in Payne, G. (ed) 2020 'Land rights and innovation: Improving tenure security for the urban poor' ITDG Publishing, Rugby, UK.

Payne, G. 2020 '*Land rights and innovation: Improving tenure security for the urban poor*' ITDG Publishing, Rugby, UK.

Ryan-Collins, J., T. Lloyd, L.Macfarlane 2021, "*Rethinking the Economics of Land and Housing*", Zed Books, London, UK.

Silas, J. 1984 "*The Kampong Improvement Programme of Indonesia: A Comparative Case Study of Jakarta and Surabaya*" in Payne, G. (ed) 'Low Income Housing in the Developing World: The Role of Sites and Services and Settlement Upgrading', Wiley, Chichester, UK.

Swan, P., E. Wegelin, K. Panchee 1983 "*Management of Sites and Services Schemes*", Wiley, Chichester, UK,

UN-Habitat (2021) '*The Role of Land in Achieving Adequate and Affordable Housing*' Nairobi. https://unhabitat.org/sites/default/files/2021/09/the_role_of_land_in_adequate_housing_final.pdf (accessed Dec.2022)

World Bank, 2015, "*Building Regulation for Resilience: Managing Risks for Safer Cities*", World Bank, Washington DC, USA.

Wakely, P. 2018 '*Housing in developing cities: Experience and Lessons*' Routledge, Taylor and Francis, New York, USA & London, UK.

Wakely, P. & S. Matararachchi 2021 '*Sustainable Community Governance and Management of Urban Housing and Local Environment*', Town Planning Review, Liverpool University Press, Liverpool, UK.

5 Legislation, norms and standards

The effective introduction of new goals and objectives to address the existential dangers of global heating and apply the lessons learnt from the 2021–23 COVID-19 pandemic to the planning, management and administration of supports to urban low-income group housing will, in many countries, require careful and widespread adjustments to prevailing urban (municipal and some national) norms and statutory regulations and guidelines. These, *inter alia*, will embrace: security of tenure and title to urban land (UN-Habitat 2021); the entitlement and management of community facilities and common open space (Max Locke Centre 2005); and safe construction methods and materials. The Government of Indonesia Kampung Improvement Programme in the cities of Jakarta and Surabaya, both subject to periodic and intensifying flooding in the 1970–80s, addressed the integrated political and managerial complexity of all these issues through the engagement of different 'levels' of government agencies, NGOs and community organisations—the principle of subsidiarity (Silas 1984, pp.69–88).

5.1 Land rights, title and tenure

As indicated in Chapter 3, neither households nor the neighbourhood communities, of which they are part, will invest their energies or resources in their dwellings or the common land that they share if the security of their right to their land, or their share in common land,[1] is not widely and officially recognised and secure (UNCHS 1997). Therefore, inalienable security to land is of paramount importance to its development and use. Throughout the world, the security of tenure to urban land takes many different forms, embracing statutory title, commonly held traditional understandings of rights and customs and religious doctrine (Payne 2002, pp.3–23). Therefore, there is a need to ensure that all such forms of land title and tenure are protected by their enshrinement in law that protects the rights of both women and men to own, rent and use the land on which they live, socialise or work, individually and collectively. In many countries such legislation, covering extended areas of land designated for

DOI: 10.4324/9781003465546-5

communal activities and facilities, is likely to be innovatory, complex and open to corruption by wealthy and politically/administratively powerful elites. Thus, all property-related legislation, and changes to it, must be open, readily accessible and understandable to all (McAuslan 1985). In essence, it is important that statutory standards, controls and guidelines are formulated *proscriptively*, setting performance limits that should not be exceeded, allowing flexibility for innovation and the incorporation of customary norms, rather than prescriptive rules that rigidly stipulate precisely and in detail what is to be done.[2]

5.2 Urban land & housing markets

Since the global financial crisis of 2008–09, there has been increasing international debate on the economic role of land as an underlying component of wider capital markets and investments—questioning the relationship between its social use in providing shelter as a home and its value as a financial security. Beyond providing household security, urban land and housing, even in low-income group neighbourhoods, has become a marketable commodity (Madden & Marcuse 2016, pp.15–52).[3] In the USA, the commodification of urban land and housing led to significant price and cost increases of housing, which traditionally had been affordable to lower-income groups, and an increase of capital trading in subprime[4] housing loans that sparked the global financial crisis [5] and to urban homelessness, social deprivation and poverty worldwide.

Case Study 2   Informal housing market mechanisms in Aleppo, Syria, 2011–21

The ancient city of Aleppo (حلب *Halab*), which, by the dawn of the twenty-first century, had a population of c.2.4 million growing at 3 percent p.a. Some 45 percent of the city's population lived in informal settlements that, in turn, were growing at 4 percent p.a.

In the decade prior to the civil war in Syria, as with land values, the prices paid for ('illegally' built) houses in informal settlements in Aleppo varied widely. They depended more on the location and the perceived level of security against eviction than on the quality of construction. For example, in 2009, two-story houses with no formal land title or building licence on plots of 100–150m² sold for between US$10,00–15,000.[6] Properties in informal settlements but with formally recognised title to the plot of land and an approved building licence could fetch up to three times these prices, or more. Due to a tradition of caution in this volatile informal property market, risk-averse vendors would not allow purchasers to occupy a house until it was fully paid for, so most buyers had to come with ready cash, though on occasions a vendor might accept payment in two or three instalments. As no formal housing finance agencies existed, house buyers had to rely on borrowing from family or other members of their community to augment their savings for house purchase.

Figure 5.1 Aleppo, Syria: legally registered house in Haydariya informal settlement, built by the owner's family, engaging local building-trade artisans, over a period of 12 years to a high standard of construction and finishes, up for sale at a relatively high price, in the local informal housing market

(Photo: Patrick Wakely, 2009)

Trade in eviction (warning) notices

In anticipation of the demolition of property in informal settlements either because of their illegality or intentions to redevelop the area, formally, the municipality or government issued notices to affected households, warning them of their pending eviction. This entitled the recipients to official re-housing or the award of a plot of land in the formal sector,[7] which hitherto had been highly subsidised. Thus, the warning of an eviction notice was also a promissory note entitling the holder to formally recognised property when the eviction and demolition ultimately took place. In opportunistic response, a significant 'virtual' market in 'property futures' developed through the speculative buying and selling of official eviction notices, locally known as 'warning papers' or 'entitlement notices'.

Experience showed that there was often a substantial time lag, on occasion of many years, between the 'intention to evict' and issue of the 'warning notices' and the actual eviction, or it did not even happen in the affected householder's lifetime. On the other hand, it was also shown that when it did take place, there were significant rewards to be gained from the entitlement to formal housing. However, there were also costs, as new social housing did not come free; beneficiaries had to pay a significant proportion of its cost that many low-income families were unable to meet. So those recipients of 'warning notices', who estimated that they would be unable to meet the cost of official housing, or those in need of ready cash for investment in an enterprise or simply to defray the cost of living, sold their 'entitlement notices' to the highest bidder. They gambled on being able to stay in their house for many years before having to re-house themselves by buying, renting or squatting in another informal settlement. The purchaser gambled on an early eviction/demolition so that he could claim his newly acquired property, or could sell on the 'entitlement notice' to a higher bidder. The older the notice, the higher was its value, on the assumption that its redemption date would be closer. As soon as there were signs of demolition or other development on the ground, or someone gained any 'insider information' of plans to start work, the value of 'notices' increased rapidly. 'Warning notices' often changed hands many times before they were redeemed.

For example, in 2007 a property owner in the north of Haydariya neighbourhood paid US$3,000[8] (SYP150,000) for his entitlement, knowing that it had been bought and sold four times since the original (authentic) recipient sold it for US$10,000[2] five years earlier. Another example stemmed from 2004 when the municipality announced its intention to clear the entire informal settlement of Tal Al-Sawda following the collapse of several buildings due to unstable soil conditions. It issued 'eviction notices' that commanded a relatively high price, because of the seeming urgency of the project. One recipient immediately sold his 'warning paper' to an agent for US$2,000[2] (SYP 100,000) and bought a Suzuki mini-truck in order to supplement his livelihood. Four years later, when the warning papers could finally be redeemed for a plot of land to the north of Haydariya, it was bought for US$10,000² (SYP500,000) by a merchant who built a substantial three-story building with a basement and roof terrace that was valued atUS$12,000² in 2009.

Informal real estate agents

Real estate agents operated in all the established informal settlements. Generally, they were leaders in their community, and the brokering of property deals was only part of their social or governance role, an important function of which was arbitrating in disputes, most of which were over property rights. Some real estate agents were responsible for negotiating the acquisition of land for Haydariya settlement when it was first developed. A few were purely commercial deal brokers with no apparent attachment to the neighbourhood or other function in the community.

The buying and selling of properties that do not have legal documents was always done through agents who were central to the 'proof of purchase' and the settlement of disputes in the absence of any formal documentation of the transfer. They also played an important role in the letting of rented property, particularly in commercial and industrial lettings. However, they were also engaged in residential lettings, especially where there was the possibility of disputes over rent payments for which they took responsibility for arbitration.

Rarely did they get involved in dealings, either formal or informal, with government or municipal authorities. These were left to the vendors and purchasers, though an agent sometimes made introductions on the behalf of his 'clients'. The only sale transactions that did not go through the intermediary of an agent were those between members of the same family or close and trusted friends.

As with the sale of land, informal agents took a commission of between 3 and 5 percent of the sale price of houses that they brokered, generally shared half-and-half between the vendor and purchaser. Higher commissions, often as a flat fee rather than a percentage of the transaction cost, were paid for arranging the transfer of informal commercial and industrial properties.

For arranging tenancies in rental property, agents generally charged a fixed fee that represented the equivalent of one month's rent for 'leases' of more than one year's duration.

All real estate agents emphasised the importance of 'formalising' the informal settlements. They claimed that the quality of buildings and the environment in general would be vastly improved if people had recognised title to their houses and workplaces, invariably drawing on actual examples, pointing out that the value of property would therefore increase significantly—as would their fee rates!

This case study has shown that the property market in the well-established medium-density informal settlements in Aleppo was not static, though, in the prevailing economic and legislative climate, was not particularly vibrant either. Nevertheless, there was a self-regulating system of market management that was efficient and worked well, serving equally the buyers, sellers and renters of property. However, due to market demand for low-income housing and the lack of effective development control measures, there was a danger of these settlements becoming 'overdeveloped' in terms of the subdivision of small plots and the vertical construction of additional floors, thereby posing a threat to public health and safety that did not exist at the time. It seemed important that any legislative measures to regulate development in informal settlements and/or to 'formalise' property titles did not upset the apparent smooth working of the market.

However, it all came to an end with the destruction caused by the civil war in Syria[9] and its aftermath, in which national legislation deemed all urban informal settlements 'illegal' and entitling developers, contracted to clear war-damage rubble and redevelop the land, to demolish informal settlements and develop the land commercially.

Notes

1 Shared ownership of commons is made increasingly significant by the threat of pathogen transmission.
2 Prescriptive instructions may be appended to proscriptive guides as illustrative 'deemed-to-satisfy' ("such as") examples of acceptable performance.
3 Even to the extent of an explicit retail, private sector, market in "*buy-to-let*" single residential properties in towns and cities the UK.
4 High-risk, un-secured loans to householders with 'low credit-rating'.
5 Initiated by the bankruptcy of the American investment bank, 'Lehman Brothers' in 2008.
6 SYP 500,000–750,000
7 Somewhere in the city; not necessarily close to their current informal dwelling
8 Exchange rate in 2010: US$ (50 Syrian pounds = US$1[00])
9 Civil conflict was started in Syria by the occupants of informal settlements in Damascus making demands for the secure formal recognition of title to the urban land on which they lived. This escalated into the country's joining the

'Arab Spring' of political reform, initiated in Tunisia, followed by Libya and Egypt, then taken up by the Da'esh (Al-qaida, ISIS) political and military movement in conflict with the brutally intransigent Syrian government and armed forces, led by President Bashar Al Assad, with international military assistance.

References

Beall, J. 2005 *'Funding local governance: Small grants for democracy and development'*, ITDG Publishing, Rugby, UK.

Cifuentes-Faura, J. 2022 *'European policies and their role in combating climate change over the years'*, Air Quality, Atmosphere and Health, Vol.15, pp.1333–1340, Springer, Cham, Switzerland, https://link.springer.com/article/10.1007/s11869-022-01156-5#article-info (accessed Feb.2023).

Madden, D. & P. Marcuse 2016 *'In defense of housing'*, Verso, London, UK.

Max Locke Centre 2005 *'The rough guide to community asset management'*, MLC Press, University of Westminster, London, UK.

McAuslan, P. 1985 *'Urban land and shelter for the poor'*, Earthscan, London, UK.

Payne, G. 2020 *'Land rights and innovation: Improving tenure security for the urban poor'*, ITDG Publishing, Rugby, UK.

Silas, J. 1984 *'The Kampong improvement programme of Indonesia: A comparative case study of Jakarta and Surabaya'*, in Payne, G. (ed) 'Low income housing in the developing world: The role of sites and services and settlement upgrading', Wiley, Chichester, UK.

Skovgaard, J. 2012 *'Learning about climate change: Finance ministries in international climate change politics'*, Global Environmental Politics, Vol.12, No.4, MIT Press, Cambridge MA, USA.

UNCHS 1997 *'The Istanbul declaration and the habitat agenda'*, UN Centre for Human Settlements, Nairobi, Kenya.

UN-Habitat 2021 *'Cities and climate change: Global report on human settlements 2011'*, Earthscan, London, UK.

6 Financial support and the way ahead

At the UN Conference of the Parties (COP21) of the United Nations Intergovernmental Panel on Climate Change (IPCC),[1] held in Paris in 2015, 196 national 'parties' negotiated and endorsed the 'Paris Agreement on climate change mitigation, adaptation, and finance'. Its key resolution was that all countries would confine global heating to 1.5–2.0°C above pre-industrial levels. To do so, it also recommended to limit the extraction and combustion of CO_2-emiting fossil fuels[2] and to investment in 'green' energy generation.[3] COP21 was preceded by, and embraced, the Montreal Protocol.[4] It was followed by a series of annual COP conferences to monitor progress in the implementation of the Paris Agreement. At COP27 in Sharm El Sheikh, Egypt, in 2022, several island nations announced the 'Rising Nations Initiative' that emphasised that many small island countries, the very existence of which are threatened by rising sea levels and ocean storms and cyclones,[5] did not have the financial or technical resources to meet their commitments to implementing the Paris Agreement—an issue, also debated by the IPCC in 2021, with regard to many African countries. In response, the delegations supported a proposal[6] for financial support to be allocated by 'western, developed countries' to the 'least-resourced developing countries' to meet their commitments. Subsequently, the Asian Development Bank (ADB) committed grant funding for this purpose within the Asian region.

6.1 Financing urban social housing adaptation

Applying the principle of subsidiarity, introduced in Chapter 1, national governments should allocate responsibility for the formulation and administration of climate change policies at national ministerial level. In many countries, climate change strategies are seen as a drain on their national economies, and responsibility for reducing them is given to the Ministry of Finance (Skovgaard

DOI: 10.4324/9781003465546-6

2012). This outlook needs to be reversed to one, such as in those countries that have established progressive, forward-looking Ministries of Environment (Diversity) and Climate Change Affairs, as in most European countries[7] that respect and support the spirit and intentions of the Paris Agreement responsibly (Cifuentes-Faura 2022), as does the UK Department (Ministry) of Energy and Climate Change (DECC).[8]

In addition to its responsibility for the formulation of national environmental and climate change policies and representing them on the all-important global stage, such a national-level institution (Ministry) should administer a fund that would be disbursed to regional or urban (municipal) authorities, to be further disbursed on a project-by-project basis to organised communities and (municipal) urban development agencies, for the implementation of approved communal environmental improvement works, and/or to cover the post-COVID-19 and climate change aspects of new social housing programmes and projects, perhaps, with international financial backing, as proposed by the 'Rising Nations Initiative', endorsed at COP27. In some developing countries, though, such external financial devolution can present patronage and accountability problems (Beall 2005, pp.1–56), which are remedied in partnerships of responsible local governments and capable CBOs, as outlined in Chapter 2.

6.2 Local management and technical supports

Returning to the discourse on community participation and partnership in Chapter 2, there is substantial evidence throughout the world that even in some of the most capable and effectively managed low- and middle-income group neighbourhood-based communities, there is a need to introduce and support an understanding of the issues and impact of global and local climate change and pathogenic transmission and avenues to their mitigation and redress. While it is likely that in many situations local or international NGOs, working with them, will take on the appropriate capacity-building tasks together with local (municipal) government agencies, and private sector professional consultants (e.g. for urban planning and design and/or landscape planning and planting), national government support funds should be made dispensable to cover the cost of such activities.[9] In these circumstances, the distinction between risk- and benefit-sharing partnerships and the participation of resident's CBOs in government-led programmes and projects (outlined in Chapter 2) becomes blurred. This ambiguity is illustrated by the highly successful example of the participatory administration of the Pablo Sexto Segundo Etapa housing estate in Bogotá, Colombia (see Case Study 3 subsequently).

Case Study 3   Subsidiarity and participation in public social housing in Bogotá, Colombia

Figure 6.1 Pablo VI-2 low-middle income group public housing estate, Bogotá, Colombia

(Photo: Jacobo Arya, 2023)

Pablo VI Segunda Etapa (PabloVI-2) is a low-middle-income group public housing estate, which has a total population of 6,500 (plus a daily floating population of c.1,800). It was designed and constructed by the Colombian national housing agency, Instituto de Crédito Territorial (ICT), in the 1970s. Located to the west of the commercial centre of the city, it is bounded on the east by an upper-middle-income group housing estate, named PabloVI,[10] also designed and constructed by ICT, a decade earlier, in the 1960s. The estate, which covers 13 hectares, is a short distance from a centre of national government administrative offices[11] and the National University of Colombia, both large employers of, *inter alia*, middle- to low-ranking clerical officers, many of whom live in PabloVI-2. Many middle-ranking police officers and their families also live on the estate.

Figure 6.2   PabloVI-2 basketball court and small-group meeting platform beneath the trees, on right

(Photo: Luz Stella Echeverri, 2022)

Figure 6.3   PabloVI-2 semi-public open space between apartment blocks

(Photo: Luz Stella Echeverri, 2022)

The title to the land of the estate is vested in a CBO, locally known as 'The Administration',[12] which represents the entire population[13] of PabloVI-2. The occupants of each of the 54 blocks of apartments are represented on 'The Administration' by an elected member. (See Note 14 later), which shows that this low-middle income group public social housing estate is an outstanding working example of the devolution of authority and the principle of subsidiarity in local environmental governance and administration and of engaging citizens in understanding and contributing to the mitigation and redress of global climate change, at marginal or no personal cost to themselves.

Figure 6.4 PabloVI-2 large landscaped open space

(Photo: Luz Stella Echeverri, 2022)

Figure 6.5 PabloVI-2, view from inside a
second-floor apartment

(Photo: Patrick Wakely, 2023)

There are 54 blocks of apartments—each five stories high, the majority with two ground-level entrances (one at each end of the rectangular blocks of apartments), giving access to stairs leading to landings on each floor, of which are the entrances to two apartments. Thus, each entrance and staircase leads to ten apartments (i.e. there are 20 apartments in the majority of the blocks). There are some longer blocks located near the commercial centre of PabloVI-2 Estate, with three entrances and staircases each serving two apartments per floor, many with commercial premises (shops, cafés, etc.) at ground-floor level.

There are 123 block representatives of 'The Administration', who may be elected in several ways, the most common of which is for him/her to be drawn from a particular entrance/staircase group of apartments, either by a whole-block election, or on a previously agreed cycle of turns. (The importance of the entrance/staircase 'level' of representation is that they are located at different ends of the rectangular blocks, thereby command-ing oversight of the adjoining public green open (recreation) space or car parking spaces, shared with neighbouring blocks.) The incumbent block representatives of 'The PabloVI-2 Administration' also hold the position of chair of their 'block administration'.[14]

Notes

1 The UN IPCC, was established, with the agreement of 154 Member States at the UN Conference on Environment and Development (UNCED), the Earth Summit, in Rio de Janeiro, Brazil in 1992. It was legally and operationally supported by the Kyoto Protocol, agreed in 1997 that commits state parties to reduce greenhouse gas emissions, based on the scientific consensus that global warming is occurring and that human-made CO_2 emissions are driving it,

2 i.e. Impacting on heavy manufacturing industries, which are major contrib-utors to the national economies of many countries.

3 Renewable energy that comes from sources that are constantly and naturally renewed, such as wind power and solar energy. Renewable energy is also often called sustainable energy. Renewable energy sources are the opposite of fossil fuels, such as oil, coal and gas, all of which are finite resources.

4 The Montreal Protocol (1987) on Substances that Deplete the Ozone Layer is the landmark multilateral environmental agreement that regulates the pro-duction and consumption of nearly 100 man-made chemicals referred to as ozone depleting substances (ODS) https://unep.org (accessed Feb2023).

5 See: https://climatemobility.org (accessed Feb2023)).

6 The proposal was presented by the Danish and Scottish delegates.

7 Coordinated by the EU Environment Council that administers the EU Envi-ronment Law, which includes climate change policies and performance targets.

8 In 2016 the DECC merged with the UK Department (Ministry) for Business Innovation & Skills to form the UK Business, Energy and Industrial Strat-egy (BEIS).

9 See Chapter 1, Note 5, (page??)

10 Named in honour of the visit of Pope Paul VI to Bogotá in 1968.

11 CAN (Centro de Administración Nacional).

12 'La Administración'

13 1,208 residential apartments + 44 shops and other small/medium commer-cial enterprises.

14 The hierarchy of 'levels' of authority, starting with the 'lowest' is as follows:

1. Apartment. the householder has full, independent leasehold tenure to his/her apartment, which he/she may freely sell or lease and may make

non-structural changes to room layouts, fixtures, etc. but not to changes that will impact on the exterior aspect of the block (e.g. changing windows), without authorisation of The PabloVI-2 Administration;

2. Entrance/Staircase group of apartments is responsible agreeing and paying for cleaning and redecorating their entrance and staircase, but has no other administrative responsibility, except in the appointment of the Block Representative to The PabloVI-2 Administration, as outlined earlier;

3. Block Administration is responsible for collecting and accounting the Block's financial dues to the structural maintenance of the block building, and for the block's share of the maintenance and management of the public spaces and facilities of the entire PabloVI-2 Estate, as determined and accounted for by 'The Administration' (which employs a team of clerical and accounting staff);

4. PabloVI-2 Estate Administration is responsible for the maintenance and management of the public spaces and facilities of the entire PabloVI-2 Estate (including its landscaping, planting and pruning), and for Security on the Estate, including controlling traffic barriers, at entrances to the Estate, etc.

References

Beall, J. 2005 '*Funding local governance: Small grants for democracy and development*', ITDG Publishing, Rugby, UK.

Cifuentes-Faura, J. 2022 '*European policies and their role in combating climate change over the years*', Air Quality, Atmosphere and Health, Vol.15, pp.1333–1340, Springer, Cham, Switzerland, https://link.springer.com/article/10.1007/s11869-022-01156-5#article-info (accessed Feb.2023).

Skovgaard, J. 2012 '*Learning about climate change: Finance ministries in international climate change politics*', Global Environmental Politics, Vol.12, No.4, MIT Press, Cambridge MA, USA.

UN-Habitat 2011 '*Cities and climate change: Global report on human settlements 2011*', Earthscan, London, UK.

Postscript

Since the late 1980s, there has been a 'globalisation' of low-income group CBOs in partnerships with local government, preoccupied with affordable urban housing, health and environmental issues, including the impacts of global climate change and pandemic pathogenic transmission, notably influenza viruses and coronavirus (Wakely 2018, p.150). An important function of all such international cooperative and exchange movements in establishing and maintaining the 'new normal' urban social housing policies and implementation strategies must be the development and proliferation of operational capacity building, embracing each of its three components: (1) human resource development; (2) organisational development; and (3) institutional development (Ibid. pp.145–149).

In order to reinforce the efficacy of all such capacity-building measures, there is an urgent need to persuasively strengthen and extend the evidence base, through the compilation, analysis and dissemination of successful and innovative operational strategies for the production, maintenance and management of urban social housing by participatory partnerships, embracing measures for the mitigation and redress of the impact of global climate change and the control and eventual elimination of harmful viral transmissions (Kennedy 2023), gleaned from the lessons learned from the 2021–23 coronavirus pandemic and other recent regional and global crises (Omand 2023, pp.40–68, 185–189, 279–315).[1]

Note

1 In April 2023, the United Nations World Health Organisation (WHO) reported the onset of a proliferation of extensive regional epidemics of cholera, affecting more than 1 billion people worldwide, with isolated cases occurring even in northern Europe, including one in the UK (where the last reported case of cholera was in London in 1866); and warning of the possibility of its imminent spreading into a global Cholera Pandemic.

DOI: 10.4324/9781003465546-7

References

Kennedy, J. 2023 '*Pathogenesis: How germs made history*', Transworld Digital, London, UK.

Omand, D. 2023 '*How to survive a crisis: Lessons in resilience and avoiding disaster*', Penguin/Random House, London, UK.

Wakely, P. 2018 '*Housing in developing cities: Experience and lessons*', Routledge/Taylor and Francis, New York, USA & London, UK.

Bibliography
Published in English

Abbott, J. 1996 'Sharing the city: Community participation in urban manage-ment', Earthscan, London, UK.

Abrams, C. 1964 'Housing in the modern world: Man's struggle for shelter in an urbanising world', MIT Press, Cambridge, MA, USA.

ACHR 2004 'Negotiating the right to stay in the city', Environment & Urbani-zation, Vol.16, No.1, Sage, London, UK.

ADB 2005 'Providing affordable housing for the urban poor in Philip-pines', http://www.adb.org/media/Articles/2003/3958_Philippines_Urban_ Housing/ (accessed Aug.2016).

Adedeji, D.S. & Olufemi, A. n.d. 'Planning policies and affordable housing in Nigeria: An analysis of Abuja master plan scheme and the re-validation of certificate of occupancy', www.york.ac.uk/inst/chp/hsa/autumn04/daramola. pdf (accessed Sept.2016).

Alberti, M. 2008 'Advances in urban ecology—integrating human and ecologi-cal processes in urban ecosystems', Springer Science, New York.

Alimuddin, S., A. Hasan & A. Sadiq 2004 'The work of the Anjuman Samaji Behbood in Faisalabad, Pakistan', in Mitlin, D. & D. Satterthwaite (eds) 'Empowering squatter citizen: Local government, civil society and urban poverty reduction', Earthscan, London, UK.

Allen, A. & N. You (eds) 2002 'Sustainable urbanisation: Bridging the Green and Brown agendas', Development Planning Unit (DPU), University Col-lege London (UCL), London, UK.

Angel, S. & T. Chirathamkijkul 1983 'Slum reconstruction: Land sharing as an alternative to eviction in Bangkok', in Angel, S. et al. (eds) 'Land for housing the poor', Select Books, Singapore.

Archer, D. & S. Boonyabancha 2011 'Seeing a disaster as an opportunity: Har-nessing the energy of disaster survivors for change', Environment & Urbani-zation, Vol.23, No.2, Sage, London, UK.

Arnstein, S.R. 1969 'A ladder of citizen participation', Journal of the American Institute of Planners, Vol.35, No.4, Washington, DC, USA.

Atkinson, A. 2009 'Climate change policy, energy and cities', International Journal of Urban Sustainable Development, Vol.1, No.1–2, Taylor and Fran-cis, Abingdon, UK and New York, USA.

Audefroy, J.F. 2011 'Haiti: Post earthquake lessons learned from traditional construction', Environment & Urbanization, Vol.23, No.2, Sage, London, UK.

Badami, M. 2023 *Compressed natural gas buses in India: Seeing through the air pollution lens, darkly*. Seminar presentation, UCL Development Planning Unit, June.

Bajracharya, B.N. 1995 '*Promoting small towns for rural development: A view from Nepal*', Asia-Pacific Population Journal, Vol.10, Delhi, India.

Bakhtyar, B., A. Zaharim, K. Sopiam & S. Moghimi 2013 '*Housing for poor people: A review on low-cost housing process in Malaysia*', WSEAS Transactions on Environment & Development, http://www.wseas.org/multimedia/journals/environment/2013/5715-106.pdf (accessed Nov.2016).

Banks, N. 2008 '*A tale of two wards: Political participation and the urban poor in Dhaka City*', Environment & Urbanization, Vol.20, No.2, Sage, London, UK.

Beall, J., O. Crankshaw & S. Parnell 2002 '*Uniting a divided city: Governance and social exclusion in Johannasburg*', Earthscan, London, UK.

Bebbington, A., S. Hickey & D. Mitlin (eds) 2008 '*Can NGOs make a difference? The challenge of development alternatives*', Zed Books Ltd, London, UK and New York, USA.

Biel, R. 2000 '*The new imperialism*', Zed Books. London, UK.

Biel, R. 2012 '*The entropy of capitalism*', Brill, Leiden, Netherlands.

Bogdanov, A. 1996 1913–17 *Bogdanov's Tektologia [original title: The universal science of organisation (Tektologia)]*, Hull, UK: Centre for Systems Studies Press.

Boughton, J. 2018 '*Municipal dreams: The rise and fall of council housing*', Verso, London, UK.

Boxall, S. 2018 '*The London plan—doomed to fail because it's impossible to deliver?*', Nov.11, https://stevenboxall.wordpress.com/2018/11/11/the-london-plan-doomed-to-fail-because-its-impossible-to-deliver/.

Brown, G. 2021 '*Seven ways to change the world*', Simon and Schuster, London, UK.

Buckley, R.M. & J. Kalarickal (eds) 2006 '*Thirty years of world bank shelter lending, what have we learned?*', World Bank, Washington, DC, USA.

Buckley, R.M., A. Kallergis & L. Wainer 2016 '*Addressing the housing challenge: Avoiding the Ozmandias syndrome*', Environment & Urbanization, Vol.28, No.1, London, UK.

Burra, S. 1999 '*Resettlement and rehabilitation of the urban poor: The story of Kanjur Marg*', DPU Working Paper No.99, UCL, London, UK.

Business in the Community 2010 http://www..btc.org.uk/resources/case_studies (accessed Aug.2016).

Chana, T. 1984 '*Nairobi: Dandora and other projects*' in Payne, G.K. (ed) 'Low-Income housing in the developing world: The role of sites and services and settlement upgrading', Wiley, Chichester, UK.

Chant, S. 2013 '*Cities through a "gender lens": A golden "urban age" for women in the Global South*', Environment & Urbanization, Vol.25, No.1, Sage, London, UK.

CHF 2004 '*Strategic assessment of the affordable housing sector in Ghana*', CHF International, Silver Spring, MD, USA.

Choguill, C.L. 1995 '*The future of planned urban development in the third world: New directions*', in Aldrich, B. & R. Sandhu (eds) 'Housing the urban poor: Policy and practice in developing countries', Zed Books, London, UK.

Choudry, A. 2015 *Learning activism—the intellectual life of contemporary social movements*, University of Toronto Press, Toronto.

Cities Alliance 2006 '*Guide to city development strategies: Improving urban performance*', Cities Alliance, Washington, DC, USA.

Cohen, M. 1983a '*The challenge of replicability: Towards a new paradigm for urban shelter in developing countries*', Regional Development Dialogue, Vol.4, No.1, pp.90–99, Nagoya, Japan.

Cohen, M. 1983b '*Learning by doing: World Bank lending for urban development 1972–82*', The World Bank, Washington, DC, USA.

Cohen, M. 2007 '*Aid, density and urban form: Anticipating Dakar*', Built Environment, Vol.33, No.2, Alexandrine Press, Oxford, UK.

Cooper, J. & C. Isendahl 2014 '*Thinking back to look ahead*', Global Environmental Change, No.83, Elsevier, Amsterdam, Netherlands.

Cotton, A. & R. Franceys 1991 '*Services for shelter*', Liverpool Planning Manual 3, Liverpool University Press, Liverpool, UK.

Cotton, A. & M. Sohail 1997 '*Community partnered procurement: A socially sensitive option*', Waterlines: International Journal of Appropriate Technologies for Water Supply and Sanitation, Vol.16, No.2, ITDG Publishing, Rugby, UK.

D'Cruz, C. & D. Satterthwaite 2005 '*Building homes, changing official approaches: The work of urban poor organisations and their federations and their contributions to meeting the millennium development goals*', IIED Poverty Reduction in Urban Areas Working Paper 16, London.

D'Monte, D. (ed) 2006 '*Mills for sale: The way ahead*', Marg Publications, Mumbai, India.

De Soto, H. 2001 '*The mystery of capital*', Finance and Development, Vol.38, No.1, IMF, Washington, DC, USA.

E&U (ed) 2007–2008 '*Finance for low-income housing and community development*' and '*Finance for housing, livelihoods and basic services*', Environment & Urbanization Vol.19, No.2 and Vol.20, No.1, Sage, London, UK.

E&U 2009 '*Getting land for housing: What strategies work for low-income groups?*', Environment & Urbanization Brief, No.19, London, UK.

E&U (ed) 2015 '*Sanitation and drainage in cities*', Environment & Urbanization, Vol.27, No.1–2, Sage, London, UK.

ENDA-RUP 2005 '*Parcelles assainies*', http://www.hicnet.org/document.php?pid=2611.

Ferguson, B. & J. Navarete 2003 '*A financial framework for reducing slums: Lessons from experience in Latin America*', Environment & Urbanization, Vol.15, No.2, Sage, London, UK.

Fernandes, E. 2010 '*The city statute and the legal urban order*' in 'The city statute of Brazil: A commentary', Cities Alliance, Washington, DC, USA.

Fernandes, E. 2011 '*Regularization of informal settlements in Latin America*', Policy Focus Report Series, Lincoln Institute of Land Policy, Cambridge, MA, USA.

Fiori, J. & J. Brandao 2012 '*Spatial strategies and urban social policy: Urbanism and poverty reduction in the Favelas Rio de Janeiro*', in Hernandez, F., L. Allen & P. Kellett (eds) '*Rethinking the informal city: Critical perspectives from Latin America*', Berghahn Books, Oxford, UK and New York, USA.

Fiori, J., H. Hinsley & L. Barth (eds) 2014 '*Housing as urbanism: Critical reflections on the Brazilian experience of urban housing*', Architectural Association, London, UK.

Fiori, J. & R. Ramirez 1992 '*Notes on the self-help housing critique*' in Mathéy, K. (ed) 'Beyond self-help housing', pp.23–31, Mansell, London, UK.

Fiori, J., E. Riley & R. Ramirez 2001 '*Physical upgrading and social integration in Rio de Janeiro: The case of Favela Bairro*', DISP The Planning Review, No.147, Zurich, Switzerland.

Fowler, A. 1998 '*Authentic NGDO partnerships in the new policy agenda for international aid: Dead end or light ahead*', Development and Change, Vol.1, No.29, Wiley, London, UK.

Frediani, A. 2007 '*Amartya Sen, the World Bank and the redress of urban poverty: A Brazilian case study*', Journal of Human Development, Vol.8, No.1, Routledge, Abingdon, UK.

Freire, M. & R. Stren (eds) 2001 '*The challenge of urban government: Polices and practices*', World Bank Institute Development Studies, Washington, DC, USA.

Freire, P. 2005a 1970 '*Pedagogy of the oppressed*', Continuum, New York, USA.

Freire, P. 2005b 1974 '*Education for critical consciousness*', Continuum, New York, USA.

Gattoni, G. 2009 '*A case for the incremental housing in sites-and-services programs*', paper presented at IDB conference, July, http://idbdocs.iadb.org/WSDocs/getDocument.aspx?DOCNUM-2062811 (accessed Nov.2016).

Geddes, M. 2000 '*Tackling social inclusion in the European Union: The limits to the new orthodoxy of local partnership*', International Journal of Urban and Regional Research, Vol.24, No.4, Wiley, London, UK.

Gibson, T. 1979 '*People power: Community and works groups in action*', Pelican, London, UK.

Gilbert, A. 2008 '*Slums, tenants and home-ownership: On blindness to the obvious*', International Development Planning Review, Vol.30, No.2, pp.i–x, Liverpool, UK.

Government of Sri Lanka (GoSL) 1983 '*Housing options and loans package (HOLP): Million houses programme*', National Housing Development Authority, Colombo, Sri Lanka.

GTZ 2009 '*Memorandum on sustainable urban development in Syria*', GTZ, mimeo, Damascus, Syria.

Guldi, J. & D. Armitage 2014 '*The history manifesto*', Cambridge University Press, Cambridge, UK.

Gunderson, L.H. & C.S. Holling (eds) 2002 '*Panarchy: Understanding transformation in human and natural systems*', Island Press, Washington, DC, USA.

Gupte, J. & D. Mitlin 2021 '*Covid-19: What is not being addressed*', Environment & Urbanization, Vol.33, No.1, Sage, London, UK.

Hamdi, N. & R. Goethert 1997 '*Action planning for cities: A guide to community practice*', John Ailey & Sons, Chichester, UK.

Hardoy, J. & D. Satterthwaite 1989 '*Squatter citizen*', Earthscan, London, UK.

Hargroves, C. et al. 2009 '*Factor five: Transforming the global economy through 80% improvements in resource productivity. A report of the club of Rome*', Earthscan, London, UK.

Harjo, J. 2002 '*A map to the next world in how we became huma: New and selected poems 1975–2001*', W.W. Norton and Company, New York, USA.

Hasan, A. 2000 '*Housing for the poor: Failure of formal sector strategies*', City Press, Karachi, Pakistan.

Hasan, A. 2009 '*Participatory development: The story of the orangi pilot project—research and training institute and urban resource centre, Karachi*', Oxford University Press, Oxford, UK.

Hastings, A. 1996 '*Unravelling the process of partnership in urban regeneration policy*', Urban Studies, Vol.33, No.2, Sage, London, UK.

Hayek, F. von. 1964 '*The theory of complex phenomena*', in Bunge, M. (ed) *The critical approach to science and philosophy*', Collier-Macmillan, London, UK.

Helming, S. & M. Göbel 1997 '*ZOPP: Objectives-oriented project planning*', GTZ, Frankfurt, Germany.

Heylighen, F. 2008 'Complexity and self-organization', in Bates, M.J. & M. Maack (eds) '*Encyclopaedia of library and information sciences*', Taylor & Francis, Abingdon, UK.

Hoonrweg, D., L. Sugar, C. Lorena & T. Gomez 2011 '*Cities and greenhouse gas emissions: Moving forward*', Environment & Urbanization, Vol.23, No.1, Sage, London, UK.

IHC (International Housing Coalition) 2008 '*Multilateral and bi-lateral funding for housing and slum upgrading development in developing countries*', IHC, Washington, DC, USA.

Imparato, I. & J. Ruster 2003 '*Slum upgrading and participation: Lessons from Latin America*', The World Bank, Washington, DC, USA.

Jenks, M. & R. Burgess (eds) 2000 '*Compact cities: Sustainable urban forms for developing countries*', Spon Press, London, UK.

Jere, H. 1984 '*Lusaka: Local participation in planning and decision-making*', in Payne, G.K. (ed) 'Low-income housing in the developing world: The role of sites and services and settlement upgrading', Wiley, Chichester, UK.

Jones, J.C. 1970 '*Design methods: Seeds of human futures*', Wiley-Interscience, London, UK.

Kearne, D.H. & S. Parriss 1982 '*Evolution of shelter programs for the urban poor: Principal findings*', World Bank Staff Working Paper, No.547, World Bank, Washington, DC, USA.

Keivani, R., M. Mattingly & H. Majedi 2008 '*Public management of urban land, enabling markets and low income housing provision: The overlooked experience of Iran*', Urban Studies, Vol.45, No.9, Sage, London, UK.

Kennedy, J. 2023 '*Pathogenesis: How germs made history*', Transworld Digital, London, UK.

Kumar, S. 1996 '*Subsistence and petty-capitalist landlords: A theoretical framework for the analysis of landlordism in third world low-income settlements*', International Journal of Urban and Regional Research, Vol.20, No.2, pp.317–329, Wiley, London, UK.

Kumar, S. 2001 '*Social relations, rental housing markets & the poor in urban India*', Department of Social Policy, LSE, London, UK.

Kumar, S. 2011 '*The research–policy dialectic: A critical reflection on the virility of landlord–tenant research and the impotence of rental housing policy formulation in the urban Global South city'*, Vol.15, No.6, pp.662–673, London, UK.

Lall, S. 2002 *'An evaluation of a public sector low-income housing project in Alwar: India'*, Working Paper 6, Society for Development Studies, New Delhi, India.

Lang, R. 2019 *'Social sustainability and collaborative housing: Lessons from an international comparative study'*, in Shirazi, M.R. & R. Keivani (eds) 'Urban social sustainability: Theory, policy and practice', Routledge, New York, USA, and Abingdon, UK.

Lankatilleke, L. 1986 *'Training and information for institutional development for the implementation of the million houses programme of Sri Lanka'*, Habitat International, Vol.10, No.3, pp.109–129. Pergamon Press, Oxford, UK.

Lee-Smith, D. & P. Memon 1988 *'Institution development for delivery of low-income housing: An evaluation of Dandora community development project in Nairobi'*, Third World Planning Review, Vol.10, No.3, pp.217–238, Liverpool, UK.

Léna, E. 2012 *'Mukhalafat in Damascus: The form of an informal settlement'*, in Ababsa, M. et al. (eds) 'Popular housing and land tenure in the Middle East', The American University in Cairo Press, Cairo, Egypt and New York, USA.

Lewis, M. & P. Conaty 2012 *'The reliance imperative: Cooperative transitions to a steady state economy'*, New Society, Gabriola Island, BC, Canada.

Lines, K., S. Dzimadzi, E. Lubega, P. Madimu-Matsangaise, V. Rao, A. Sebanja, H. Zidana & D. Mitlin 2023 *'COVID-19 vaccine rollout: Data from informal settlements in Harare, Kampala, Lilongwe and Mumbai'*, Environment & Urbanization, Vol.35, No.1, Sage, London, UK.

Lloyd-Jones, T. 2006 *'Mind the gap! Post-disaster reconstruction and the transition from humanitarian relief'*, Max Lock Centre, University of Westminster/RICS, London, UK.

Lorardoni, F. & J.C. Bolay 2016 *'Rental housing and the urban poor: Understanding the growth and production of rental housing in Brazilian Favelas'*, International Journal of Urban Sustainable Development, Vol.8, No.1, Taylor & Francis, Abingdon, UK.

Mackintosh, M. 1992 *'Partnership: Issues of policy and negotiation'*, Local Economy, Vol.7, Sage, London, UK.

Madden, D. & P. Marcuse 2016 *'In defense of housing: The politics of crisis'*, Verso, London, UK and New York, USA.

Magalhães, S. 1997 *'Pobreza Urbana, un fenómeno de la exclusion: la experiencia de Rio de Janeiro y el Programa Favela Bairro'*, Secretaria Municipal de Habitação, Rio de Janeiro, Brazil.

Mangin, W. 1967 *'Latin American squatter settlements: A problem and a solution'*, Latin American Research Review, Vol.2, pp.65–98.

Marcuse, P. 1992 *'Why coventional self-help projects won't work'*, in Mathéy, K. (ed) 'Beyond self-help housing', pp.15–21, Mansell, London, UK.

Marris, P. 1961 *'Family and social change in an African city'*, Routledge, London, UK and New York, USA.

Mason, P. 2016 *'Postcapitalism: A guide to our future'*, Penguin, London, UK.

Max Locke Centre 2005 *'The rough guide to community asset management'*, MLC Press, University of Westminster, London, UK.

McAuslan, P. 1985 '*Urban land and shelter for the poor*', Earthscan, London, UK.

McCarney, P. (ed) 1996 '*Cities and governance: New directions in Latin America, Asia and Africa*', Centre for Urban and Community Studies, University of Toronto, Toronto, Canada.

McGranahan, G. & D. Satterthwaite 2014 '*Urbanisation concepts and trends*', IIED Working Paper, IIED, London, UK.

McLeod, R. & K. Mullard 2006 '*Bridging the finance gap in housing and infrastructure*', ITDG Publishing, Rugby, UK.

Meadows, D.H. 2008 '*Thinking in systems—a primer*', Earthscan, London, UK.

Merchant, C. 1980 '*The death of nature—women, ecology and the scientific revolution*', Harper, San Francisco, USA.

MIT 2001 '*Upgrading urban communities: A resource for urban practitioners*', http://web.mit.edu/urbanupgrading/index.html (accessed Sept.2016).

Mitlin, D. 2008a '*Urban poor funds: Development by the people for the people*', IIED Poverty Reduction in Urban Areas Working Paper 18, London.

Mitlin, D. 2008b '*With and beyond the state: Co-production as a route to political influence, power and transformation for grass-roots organizations*', Environment & Urbanization, Vol.20, No.2, Sage, London, UK.

Mitlin, D. & S. Bartlett 2018 '*Editorial: Co-production n- Key ideas*', Environment & Urbanization, Vol.30, No.2, Sage, London, UK.

Mitlin, D. & D. Satterthwaite (eds) 2004 '*Empowering squatter citizen: Local government, civil society and urban poverty reduction*', Earthscan, London, UK.

Morin, E. 1992 1977 '*Method: Towards a study of humankind: The nature of nature*', Vol.1, Peter Lang, New York, USA.

Moser, C.O.N. 2016 '*Towards a nexus linking gender assets and transformational pathways in just cities*', in Moser, C.O.N. (ed) 'Gender, asset accumulation and just cities: Pathways to transformation', Routledge, Abingdon, UK and New York, USA.

Moser, C.O.N. 2017 'Gender transformation in a new global urban agenda: Challenges for habitat III and beyond', Environment & Urbanization, Vol.29, No.1, Sage, London, UK.

Moser, C.O.N. & L. Peake (eds) 1987 '*Women, Human Settlements and Housing*', Tavistock, London, UK.

Murray, M.J. 2017 '*The urbanism of exception: Global urbanism at the start of the 21st century*', pp.23–45, Cambridge University Press, Cambridge, UK.

Nelson, N. & S. Wright (eds) 1995 '*Power and participatory development: Theory and practice*', ITDG Publishing, Rugby, UK.

Omand, D. 2023 '*How to survive a crisis: Lessons in resilience and avoiding disaster*', Penguin/Random House, London, UK.

Ostby, G. 2015 '*Rural–urban migration, inequality and urban social disorder: Evidence from African and Asian cities*', Conflict Management and Peace Science, Vol.33, No.5, pp.491–515.

Ostrom, E. 2010 '*The challenge of self-governance in complex contemporary environment*', Journal of Speculative Philosophy, Vol.24, No.4, pp.316–332.

Patel, S. & D. Mitlin 2004 '*The work of SPARC, the national slum dwellers federation and Mahila Milan*', in Mitlin, D. & D. Satterthwaite (eds)

'Empowering squatter citizen: The roles of local governments and civil society in reducing urban poverty', Earthscan, London, UK.

Payne, G.K. 1984 'Introduction', in Payne, G.K. (ed) 'Low-income housing in the developing world: The role of sites and services and settlement upgrading', Wiley, Chichester, UK.

Payne, G.K., A. Durand-Lasserve & C. Rakodi 2009 '*The limits to land titling and home ownership*', Environment & Urbanisation, Vol.21, No.2, Sage, London.

Peatie, L. 1990 '*Participation: A case study of how invaders organize, negotiate and interact with government in Lima, Peru*', Environment & Urbanization, Vol.2, No.1, London, UK.

Pervaiz, A., P. Rahman & A. Hasan 2008 '*Lessons from Karachi: The role of demonstration, documentation, mapping and relationship building in advocacy for improved, urban sanitation and water services*', IIED Human Settlements Discussion Paper: Water-6, London, UK.

Phonphakdee, S., S. Visal & G. Sauter 2009 '*The urban poor development fund in Cambodia: Supporting local and citywide development*', Environment & Urbanization, Vol.21, No.2, Sage, London, UK.

Plummer, J. 2002 '*Focusing partnerships: A sourcebook for municipal capacity building in public-private partnerships*', Earthscan, London, UK.

Radjou, N. et al. 2012 '*Jugaad innovation: A frugal and flexible approach to innovation for the 21st century*', Random House, Delhi, India.

Rahman, M. 2005 'Role of NGOs in urban housing for the poor in Dhaka, Bangladesh', Global Built Environment Review, Vol.15, No.1, pp.16–29.

Rakodi, C. 2016 '*Addressing gendered inequalities in access to land and housing*', in Moser, C.O.N. (ed) 'Gender, asset accumulation and just cities: Pathways to transformation', Routledge, Abingdon, UK and New York, USA.

Ramirez, R. 2002 '*Urban poverty reduction and urban security consolidation: A new paradigm at work? A review of theory and practice*', UN-Habitat/UNDP/World Bank Urban Management Programme (UMP) Working Paper Series No.20, Nairobi, Kenya.

Redwood, M. & P. Wakely 2012 '*Land tenure and upgrading informal settlements in Colombo, Sri Lanka*', International Journal of Urban Sustainable Development, Vol.4, No.20, pp.166–186, Taylor &Francis, London, UK.

Republic of South Africa (RSA), Human Settlements Department 2012 '*Adjustments to the finance linked individual subsidy programme*', un-published, memo, Pretoria, South Africa, www.dhs.gov.za (accessed Feb.2014).

Riley, E. & P. Wakely 2005 '*Communities and communication: Building urban partnerships*', ITDG Publishing, Rugby, UK.

Robinson, J. 2013 '*The urban now: Theorising cities beyond the new*', European Journal of Cultural Studies, Vol.16, No.6, pp.659–677.

Rowbottom, S. 1990 '*Senegal case study, parcelles assaines: From project to place—after three decades*', CHF Occasional Paper, Vol.3, CHF International, Silver Spring, MD, USA.

Ryan-Collins, J., T. Lloyd & L. Macfarlane 2017 '*Rethinking the economics of land and housing*', Zed Books Ltd., London, UK.

Safier, M. 1996 '*The cosmopolitan challenge in cities on the edge of the millennium—moving from conflict to co-existence*', City, Vol.1, No.3–4, pp.12–29.

Satterthwaite, D. 2009 *'Getting land for housing: What strategies work for low-income groups'*, Environment & Urbanization, Vol.21, No.2, Sage, London, UK.

Satterthwaite, D. 2016 *'Editorial: A new urban agenda?'*, Environment & Urbanization, Vol.28, No.1, pp.3–12, Sage, London, UK.

Schlyter, A. 1995 *'Squatter and slum settlements in Zambia'*, in Aldrich, B. & R. Sandhu (eds) 'Housing the urban poor: Policy and practice in developing countries', Zed Books, London, UK.

Shirazi, M.R. & R. Keivani 2019 *'Social sustainability discourse: A critical revisit'*, in Shirazi, M.R. & R. Keivani (eds) *'Urban social sustainability: Theory, policy and practice'*, Routledge, New York, USA and Abingdon, UK.

SIDA (Swedish International Development Agency) 2007 *'Increasing access to housing and financial services: SIDA experiences in Central America'*, First Asia-Pacific Housing Forum, Singapore.

Siddiqui, T.A. 2005 *'Incremental housing development scheme (Pakistan): An innovative and successful scheme for sheltering the urban poor'*, Action Research for Shelter, Karachi, Pakistan.

Silas, J. 1984 'The Kampong improvement programme of Indonesia: A comparative case study of Jakarta and Surabaya' in, Payne, G.K. (ed) 'Low income housing in the developing world', Wiley, Chichester, UK.

Simms, D. 2010 *'Understanding Cairo: The logic of a city out of control'*, The American University in Cairo Press, Cairo, Egypt.

Sirivardana, S. 1986 *'Reflections on the implementation of the million houses programme'*, Habitat International, Vol.10, No.3, Pergamon, Oxford, UK.

Smith, R.C. 2017 *Society and social pathology: A framework for progress*, Palgrave Macmillan, London, UK.

Solana Oses, O. 2013 *'Affordable housing and urban sprawl in Mexico: The need for a paradigm shift'*, University of Manchester, Global Urban Research Centre, Briefing Paper No.4, Manchester, UK.

Stein, A. & I. Vance 2008 *'The role of housing finance in addressing the needs of the urban poor: Lessons from Central America'*, Environment & Urbanization, Vol.20, No.1, Sage, London, UK.

Suhartini, N. & P. Jones 2019 *'Urban governance and informal settlements'*, Springer, Berlin, Germany.

Tibaijuka, A.K. 2009 *'Building prosperity: Housing and economic development'*, Earthscan, London, UK.

Tipple, G. 2004 *'Settlement upgrading and home-based enterprises: Discussions from empirical data'*, Cities, Vol.21, No.5, Elsevier, Amsterdam, Netherlands.

Toye, J. 1993 *Dilemmas of development—reflections on the counter-revolution in development theory and policy*, Blackwell, Oxford, UK.

Turner, J.F.C. 1968 *'Uncontrolled urban settlement: Problems and policies'*, International Social Development Review No.1, 'Urbanization: Development Policies and Planning', United Nations, New York, USA.

Turner, J.F.C. 1972 *'Housing as A Verb'*, in Turner, J.F.C. & R. Fichter (eds) 'Freedom to build: Dweller control of the housing process', pp.148–175, Macmillan, New York, USA.

Turner, J.F.C. 1976 *'Housing by people: Towards autonomy in building environments'*, Marion Boyars, London, UK.

Turner, J.F.C. & R. Fichter (eds) 1972 '*Freedom to build: Dweller control of the housing process*', pp.148–175, Macmillan, New York, USA.

UNCHS 1991 '*The incremental development scheme: A case study of Kuda-Ki-Bustee in Hyderabad, Pakistan*', UNCHS Training Materials Series No. HS/232/91E, UN-Habitat, Nairobi, Kenya.

UN-ESCAP 1991 '*Guidelines on community-based housing finance and innovative credit systems for low-income households*', Economic and Social Commission for Asia and the Pacific, Bangkok, Thailand.

UN FAO 2008 '*Compulsory acquisition of land and compensation*', UN Food and Agriculture Organisation, FAO Land Tenure Studies No.10, Rome, Italy.

UN-Habitat 2003 revised 2010 '*The challenge of slums: Global report on human settlements 2003*', Earthscan, London, UK.

UN-Habitat 2005 '*Small loans: Shelter microfinance*', (Chapter 5) in 'Financing urban shelter: Global report on human settlements 2005', Earthscan, London, UK.

UN-Habitat 2011 '*Climate change adaptation [and mitigation] responses in urban areas*', (Chapters 5, 6) in 'Cities and climate change: Global report on human settlements 2011', Earthscan, London, UK.

UN-Habitat 2016 '*Habitat III new urban agenda*', http://habitat3.org/wp-content/uploads/N1639668-English.pdf (accessed Jan.2017).

UN Statistics Division 2021 '*Demographic yearbook 2021*', UN Department of Economic and Social Affairs, New York, USA.

United Nations 2015 '*Report of the open working group of the general assembly on sustainable development goals*', Document A/68/970, http://undocs.org/A/68/970 (accessed Jan.2018).

Valenzuela, J. & G. Vernez 1974 '*Construcción popular y estructura del Mercado de Vivienda: el Caso de Bogotá*', Revista Interamericana de Planificación, No.31, pp.88–140, Mexico.

Van der Linden, J. 1992 '*Back to the roots: Keys to successful implementation of sites-and-services*', in Mathéy, K. (ed) 'Beyond self-help housing', Mansell Publishing, London, UK.

Wakely, P. 2008 '*Land tenure in under-served settlements in Colombo, Sri Lanka*', IDRC Poverty and Environment Report Series No.6, Ottawa, Canada.

Wakely, P. 2018 '*Housing in developing cities: Experience & lessons*', Routledge, New York, USA and Abingdon, UK.

Wakely, P. 2020 '*Partnership: A strategic paradigm for the production and management of affordable housing and sustainable urban development*' International Journal of Urban Sustainable Development, Vol.12, No.1, Taylor & Francis, Abingdon, UK.

Wakely, P. & R. Abdul-Wahab 2010 '*Informal land and housing markets in Aleppo, Syria*', [English and Arabic], GiZ, Eschborn, Germany.

Wakely, P., H. Schmetzer & B. Mumtaz 1974 '*A building clinic in Baghdad*', Architectural Design, No.6(74), London, UK.

Wakely, P. & N. You (eds) 2001 '*Implementing the habitat agenda: In search of urban sustainability*', Development Planning Unit (DPU), University College London (UCL), London, UK.

Ward, C. 1973 '*Anarchy in action*', George Allen and Unwin, London, UK.

Weerapana, D. 1986 '*Evolution of a support policy of shelter: The experience of Sri Lanka*', Habitat International, Vol.10, No.3, Pergamon, Oxford, UK.

Werna, E. 1991 '*Business as usual: Small-scale contractors and the production of low-cost housing in developing countries*', Avebury Publishing, Aldershot, UK.

World Bank 1993 '*Housing: Enabling markets to work*', World Bank Policy Paper, Washington, DC, USA.

World Bank 2015 '*Building regulation for resilience: Managing risks for safer cities*', World Bank, Washington, DC, USA.

World Commission on Environment & Development 1987 '*Our common future*', (*The Bruntland Report*), Oxford University Press, Oxford, UK.

Yap, K.S. 2023 '*Upgrading informal settlements: Experiences from Asia*', White Lotus Books, Bangkok, Thailand.

Index

greenhouse gas emissions,
reduction 50
growth, engines/motors 14

Hackney, rod 27
Haydariya (Aleppo, Syria): informal
settlement *53*; neighbourhood,
entitlement payment 54–55
higher-income groups, speculative
resale 7–8
Hilldrop Area Community
Association, collaboration *47*
Hong Kong, vertical-type sea wall *39*
households, participation 21
housing: deficit 4; finance,
public provision 1; location,
determination 36–37; markets 52;
need, arithmetical figure 4; role,
perception (change) 10; units, sale
(consequence) 5
Housing and Community
Development Committees
(HCDCs), establishment 31–32
human energy/skills, contribution 30

implementation strategies 20
Indian Housing and Urban
Development Corporation
(HUDCO): income categories,
merger 7; working standard
establishment 11
Indian National Slum Dwellers
Federation (NSDF),
engagement 30
individual property holding, extent
(controls) 3
informal housing market mechanisms
(Aleppo, Syria) 52–56
informal real estate agents:
commissions 55; operation 55–56
informal sector, understanding 10
infrastructure: local infrastructure,
maintenance 25; maintenance 24;
provision 12
Instituto de Crédito Territorial
(ICT) 60
interactive learning process 16

Inter-American Development Bank
(IDB)-supported Low-Income
Settlements Programme (LISP),
evaluation 37
interdependence, value 31
inter-dependent decentralisation,
tenet 20
interim buffer zone, purpose 45
international development industry,
urbanisation (importance) 14, 15

Jacob Lines project 4
joint multilateral control 28

Karachi Development Authority,
apartment construction project 4
Khayelitsha (Cape Town), eviction/
slum clearance *6*

Ladder of Citizen Participation
(Arnstein) 27–28
ladder of progression, rungs 28
land 36; capital cost, financial
responsibility 11; inalienable
security 51–52; rights/title
51–52; tenure 51–52; tenure,
recognition 12
land development 1; cost 36–37;
residential/productive use 2
landlord, responsibility 5
landscape planning/management 43
land use 43; planning/maintenance,
participation/partnerships 44–50;
zoning/development controls 2
legislation/norms/standards 51
Lewisham Borough Council 23;
Housing Committee, self-building
approaches (adoption) 21
life-threatening heatwaves,
experience 27
Local Authority Service Delivery
Action plan (LASDAP),
implementation 32
local commercial enterprises, enabling 1
local government administrations,
climate change-induced/
geophysical hazards 43–44

For Product Safety Concerns and Information please contact our EU
representative GPSR@taylorandfrancis.com
Taylor & Francis Verlag GmbH, Kaufingerstraße 24, 80331 München, Germany

www.ingramcontent.com/pod-product-compliance
Lightning Source LLC
Chambersburg PA
CBHW061832220326
41599CB00027B/5260